ILLITERACY: A WORLD PROBLEM

Sir Charles Jeffries

ILLITERACY

A WORLD PROBLEM

FREDERICK A. PRAEGER, *Publishers*

New York · Washington · London

379.24
J 47

FREDERICK A. PRAEGER, *Publishers*
111 Fourth Avenue, New York, N.Y., 10003, U.S.A.
77–79 Charlotte Street, London, W.1, England

Published in the United States of America in 1967
by Frederick A. Praeger, Inc., Publishers

PRINTED IN GREAT BRITAIN

DEDICATION

*To all who stand outside
the gate of knowledge, unable to enter;
and to all who labour
that they may have the key*

CONTENTS

PREFACE

EVERY WRITER is also a reader, though every reader is not necessarily also a writer. A writer fondly hopes that his preface will be read before the book is begun; but as a reader he well knows that it will probably not be read at all, and that if it is read, it will probably be read after and not before the rest of the book. This, after all, is only just, for I suspect that, like myself, most writers compose their preface when the book itself has been committed to paper.

These observations are offered, not because this happens to be a book about reading and writing, but because, if it has a message (and I believe it has), that message will be found in the final chapter. That chapter written, I append an epilogue in the form of this preface, in order that, if someone who picks up the book looks, for once, at the preface first, he may feel moved, in the kindness of his heart, to glance at least at that last chapter.

This is not a whodunnit: it is more a case of who doesn't do it. Reading the end first will not spoil the story; it may even persuade those who do not know the story to discover it by reading the book in the proper progression. For it is, as they say, quite a story. It could be a triumph: it may turn out to be a tragedy.

I have had so much help from so many quarters in writing this book that I cannot adequately express my gratitude. For errors and omissions I alone am responsible, as also for any opinions offered. In dealing with so large a subject I have had to be selective and to illustrate my theme with such material as came readily to hand. If any are hurt or offended because their work has received scant mention, or no mention at all, or has been misrepresented, I sincerely ask their pardon, and would assure them that the reason is probably the same as that which led Dr Johnson to define 'pastern' as the knee of a horse: 'Ignorance, Madam, pure ignorance.'

Anything that is right in the book is due to those helpers, among whom I mention with especial gratitude Mr John Bowers who, after several years' service in the department of UNESCO concerned with literacy, is now working in the Ministry of Overseas Development and the London University Institute of Education. Nothing could exceed the kindness which Mr Bowers has shown to me, both when I visited the UNESCO headquarters in Paris in 1965 and during the writing of this book. He has generously furnished me with information and documents which I could not easily have obtained otherwise, and by his counsel has guided my amateur steps away from many pitfalls.

I also wish very warmly to thank the present director of the Literacy Division of the Department of Adult Education and Youth Activities of UNESCO, Mr Homer Kempfer, and other members of that department for letting me have copies of relevant publications and memoranda, and for giving me permission to quote from them. I owe a great debt to: the Centre de documentation pédagogique sur les pays en voie de développement of the Institut Pédagogique in Paris for papers concerning French-speaking territories; to the United States Agency for International Development for valuable reference documents; to Dr Edith Mercer, Mr A. R. G. Prosser and other members of the staff of the Ministry of Overseas Development in London for advice, encouragement and material; to Mr Peter du Sautoy of the Department of Education at Manchester University and to Dr Tom Soper of the Overseas Development Institute, both of whom helped me in finding material; to the Feed the Minds Appeal Committee, which sponsored my visit to UNESCO; to the Conference of British Missionary Societies and to the Society for Promoting Christian Knowledge for help in my survey of some aspects of the distribution problem, to the Reverend J. A. Lovejoy, formerly secretary of the Conference's Christian Literature

Council, who helped me with material; to Dr Frank C. Laubach for permission to quote from his classic writings on illiteracy; to OXFAM, Christian Aid and Educational Productions Ltd for permission to make use of their Chart of Illiteracy; and to the libraries of the Commonwealth Office and the Royal Commonwealth Society for the loan of essential books.

Finally, I would thank my brother Wilfrid for giving me the benefit of his first-hand experience, supplying detailed information about the literacy campaign which he carried out in Northern Nigeria, and contributing the Appendix; and my daughter, Mrs Daphne Topham, who did the typing.

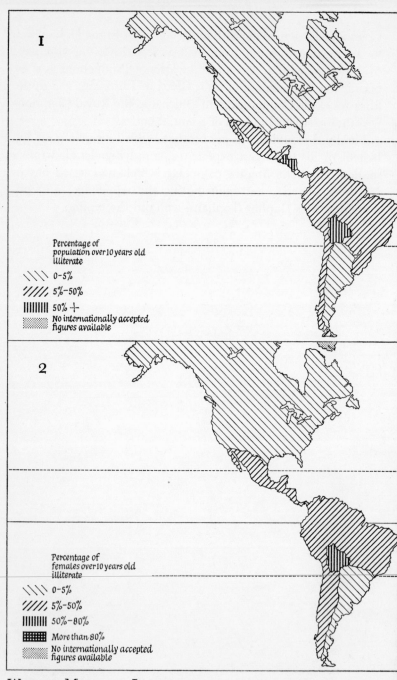

Percentage of
population over 10 years old
illiterate

\\\\ 0-5%

//// 5%-50%

|||||||| 50% +

No internationally accepted
figures available

Percentage of
females over 10 years old
illiterate

\\\\ 0-5%

//// 5%-50%

|||||| 50%-80%

More than 80%

No internationally accepted
figures available

WORLD MAPS OF ILLITERACY

1 Illiterate Proportion of Population over 10 years of age

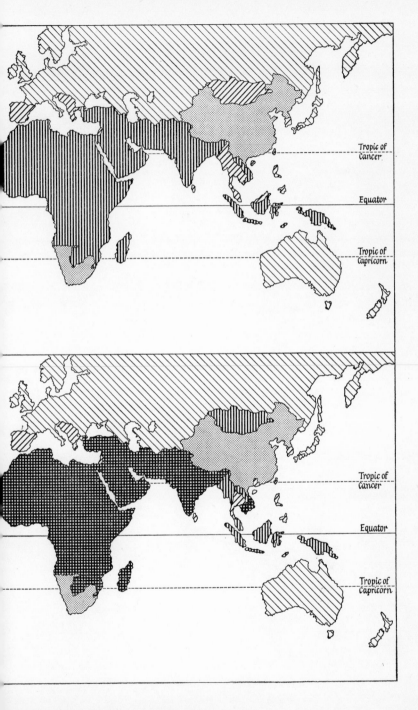

Female Illiteracy over 10 years of age

I

THE PROBLEM POSED

IN ANY modern, civilised society, reading and writing are taken for granted as indispensable elements in a person's equipment for living. Children are taught to read and write at the earliest possible age, for the rest of their education depends on their possession of the skill of literacy. The whole social, political and economic structure of the modern community rests on the assumption that every citizen can communicate, and be communicated with by means of the written or printed word.

Yet this is a comparatively recent development in human history; and it affects, so far, only certain limited areas of the world. Some two-fifths of the world's adult population—at least 700 million men and women—cannot, at the present time, read or write.* Moreover, these 'illiterates' are not evenly spread about the world but are, for the most part, concentrated in particular areas and countries. A study of the statistics prepared by UNESCO shows, at one end of the scale, a well-defined group of countries (including the United States, the Soviet Union, most of the European countries, Canada, Australia, New Zealand and Japan) in which the percentage of illiteracy is insignificant; and, at the other end, a group (including most of the countries of Africa and Asia, and several of those in Latin America) in which at least half—and in many cases more than three-quarters—of the adult population are classifiable as illiterate.[1]

To accept this as a fact is not necessarily to admit it as

* 'Adult' in this connection, usually means 'aged fifteen or over'.

constituting a 'problem'. Throughout most of its history, the human race has managed to survive, and to develop socially, morally and economically, without most of its members being able to read and write.

Certainly, the invention of reading and writing—that is to say, the use of conventional visual symbols to represent the sounds of a spoken language—goes back into the remote times of prehistory. Next to man's discovery of the art of using articulate sound to express and communicate thought, it is perhaps the most decisive and far-reaching achievement of the human mind. The pictorial images of the ancient Egyptian and Aztec civilisations, the knotted cords of the Peruvian Incas, were effective— but only up to a point: they could not possibly have become the basis of such intellectual and material advances as have been realised by the possessors of what the American historian Prescott called 'that beautiful contrivance, the alphabet'.

> It is impossible [he wrote] to contemplate without interest the struggles made by different nations, as they emerge from barbarism, to supply themselves with some visible symbol of thought—that mysterious agency by which the mind of the individual may be put in communication with the minds of a whole community. The want of such a symbol is itself the greatest impediment to the progress of civilisation. . . . Not only is such a symbol an essential element of civilisation, but it may be assumed as the very criterion of civilisation; for the intellectual advancement of a people will keep pace pretty nearly with its facilities for intellectual communications.[2]

Nevertheless—apart, perhaps, from a few special cases—even in communities which have possessed an alphabet, the knowledge and use of it have been limited throughout most of history to a particular class, and have not been diffused over the general population. It was a secret code, an instrument of power, kept in the hands of the religious and political rulers, and of those who directly served them. As social organisation became more

complex, there was a corresponding widening of the circle within which ability to read instructions and to write reports was
needed; and there was a growing appreciation of the essential
part which the written word had to play in the preservation and
dissemination of religion, culture and ideas. Even so, the spread
of literacy was a gradual process, and in the most highly developed societies its extension to the mass of the people is a fairly
recent innovation. Indeed, before the introduction of printing,
there was not much point in literacy for the great mass of the
people, for there was nothing for them to read. Hand-copied
books were scarce and expensive. Even well-to-do people customarily employed trained scribes to write for them. The Heb-
rews, whose way of life was rooted in the Scriptures, were
probably as literate as any peoples of the ancient world; but we
find in the New Testament that Jesus caused some astonishment
by his ability to read the sacred literature though not a trained
Rabbi, and his disciples were despised by the authorities as un-
lettered men. St Paul dictated his epistles, his personal post-
scripts apparently being written in a clumsy hand.

In England, in the time of the Norman kings, as in other
European countries, ability to read and write was almost entirely confined to the clergy (a term which covered numbers of
people in minor orders, as well as priests), who carried out all
the necessary legal, financial, secretarial and other paper work
for the rulers, the nobility and the merchants, most of whom
were illiterate. References to 'literate laymen' began to appear in
English records at the end of the fourteenth century, but it was
not until about two centuries later that, with the development of
grammar schools, a literate middle class came into being to meet
needs which could no longer be adequately served by church-
men. The supreme importance attached by Protestants to the
Bible was an important factor in encouraging the growth of literacy after the Reformation; but, even in the age of Milton and
Newton, not more than a 'fair proportion' of the English people
could read and write.[3] In France, according to military records,

more than half of the recruits in the army in 1832 were illiterate. In the United States, 20 per cent of the population of ten years of age and over were estimated, in 1870, to be illiterate. In Spain, as lately as 1910, over half of the people of ten years of age and over were reported as unable to read; forty years later, the percentage had dropped to 17·3, out of a much larger population.[4]

Probably in none of these, or other comparable countries, was illiteracy as such considered a 'problem', and dealt with on its own account. As social and, in particular, industrial development called for an increasing supply of educated people, schools and educational institutions came into being to meet the need; and, in due course, compulsory education of children was introduced: for example, in the United Kingdom in 1870, in France in 1882, and in most of the United States by 1900. Thus, in the long run, illiteracy faded away as successive generations of children emerged from the schools, able to read and write, until only the mentally handicapped or the few deprived by some special circumstance of the opportunity of a normal education remained without this essential skill.

In the long run: those are the significant words in the last sentence. Universal primary education is a certain and permanent recipe for the eradication of illiteracy. But it takes the best part of a century from the date of its introduction before it is possible to say that, with negligible exceptions, every adult member of the community concerned is able to read and write. In England and Wales, as lately as 1914, nearly one in a hundred of those who married signed the register by a mark. Many of these will have lived on into the 1960s, and some may never have learned even to write their names. In the summer of 1966, the London press carried reports of a voluntary movement aimed at teaching literacy to adults who, though they had been to school, were still unable to read a newspaper or to write a letter. It was estimated that the national figure for people in this state of semi-literacy might be as high as 20 per cent.

6

In the United States, it was reckoned in 1964 that 10 per cent of the population aged eighteen and over were unable even to read street signs or labels on bottles, or to fill up the application form for a job. Half a million such people lived in New York City alone. Public concern over this situation found expression in a two-day conference arranged in April 1964, by the American Book and Textbook Publishers' Councils and attended by leading official and unofficial experts. The discussions resulted in constructive proposals for the training of the illiterate people and for the provision of reading material adapted to their special needs.[5]

The problem of illiteracy in the developing countries is, however, very different from such residual problems as have yet to be finally dealt with in the lands of Europe and North America, where the elimination of illiteracy has not been, and has not needed to be, considered as a specialised operation. Before the industrial revolution of the nineteenth century, there already existed in these countries a substantial educated class; and in the urban communities considerable numbers of people, albeit not describable as educated, were literate to some extent at least. Industrial development both demanded and caused an ever-widening diffusion of education, reaching out eventually to the agricultural populations of the countryside, as well as to the industrial workers in the towns. Without the necessity or, indeed, the organisation for conscious planning, the normal play of supply and demand gradually produced the required result.

Very different is the position of a country where the people, for whose simple needs the spoken word has hitherto sufficed, suddenly find themselves involved in the policies and economics of the twentieth-century world. In such circumstances—unprecedented in the history of mankind—it is just not possible to wait until an educational system has been built up and its products gradually become available. It was probably in Russia, after the Bolshevik revolution of 1917, that it was first realised that the immediate necessity in such circumstances was not only to provide schools for the coming generations, but also to carry out a planned campaign to teach the existing adult population to read and write. Tolstoy, in the middle of the nineteenth century, estimated that not more than one per cent of his fellow-countrymen were literate. However that may have been, the census figures of 1897 showed over a quarter of the Russian people as illiterate, and when the Soviet government came to power it found that, of the various peoples under its jurisdiction, something like 80 per cent were in this category. Many members of non-Russian communities could not speak Russian, and some of the 'national minorities' had no written language at all. Lenin described illiteracy as 'Enemy Number One', and from 1920 onwards a vast operation was set on foot to eliminate it. This had such success that, by 1941, the back of the problem had been broken, and the census of 1959 could record a literacy rate of 98·5 per cent.[6]

Immense as the difficulties were in Russia, the conditions there were in certain respects favourable compared with those in some other countries. The Russian language and its treasures of literature were there as a basis; there was a strong central government which could take effective and, if necessary, drastic action. Above all, there was an upsurge of national spirit, a feeling of liberation from servitude, a general desire on the part of the people that their country should take its rightful place among the great nations, and lead the world into the Marxist Utopia.

Strong government, and the incentive of national pride, were also effective in post-Ottoman Turkey where, at the time of the revolution of 1923, only 10 per cent of the people were literate. The same factors were operative in modern China, though there the difficulties have been greater because of the peculiar characteristics of the ideographic script. But, until recently, most of the countries classed as 'major areas of illiteracy' were, directly or indirectly, dependent on one or other of the Western powers. The colonial authorities, notably those of Britain and France,

8

were by no means unaware of the need for literacy, but teaching dependent peoples to read and write was only one of the many calls on the limited resources available for the development of the social services. In fact, it was not until after the end of the Second World War that the metropolitan governments began to provide substantial funds to help in financing the economic and social progress of their dependencies; and by then the political revolution was on the way.

In the short space of less than twenty years after the Second World War, all the larger and many of the smaller territories of the colonial empires of Britain, France and Holland, together with Belgium's dependency of the Congo and the United States dependency of the Philippines, achieved national independence. They asumed the responsibilities as well as the privileges of sovereign states, becoming members of the United Nations, equal in status and voting power to the older countries. In this novel situation, the handicap of mass illiteracy, from which almost all of them suffered, assumed a new importance and urgency. Thoughtful people began to realise that illiteracy was a potent factor in international relations and had an important bearing on issues of war and peace. So long as the gap between the privileged minority and the underprivileged majority persisted and widened, there could be no stable world order. Modern communications had enabled, indeed compelled, the under-privileged to realise their condition and to resent it. The time must come when the gap would no longer be tolerated. It would be closed either by raising the less privileged to a higher standard of living or by dragging the privileged down to the level of the rest.

Such ideas no doubt struck strangely on the ears of people who had made their fortunes out of cheap labour and raw materials from the tropical countries, but their inescapable truth came increasingly to be recognised during the post-war period. 'The map of hunger and the map of illiteracy in the world are the same. The regions where people do not have enough to eat

9

are also those where they cannot read, and this is no accident. For progress is indivisible. People cannot eat more unless they produce more, and they cannot produce more without being taught.'[7]

Emancipated from colonial status, the new countries became responsible for working out their own salvation. A national spirit could now encourage their peoples to fresh efforts. But there were severe limits to what they could do on their own account. The former colonial powers, however ready and willing they might be to continue helping their former dependencies to the extent that their resources allowed and the independent governments would accept, were in no sort of position to finance the kind of programme which an effective attack on illiteracy would involve. Only international action on a massive scale could suffice. Accordingly, when the United Nations Educational, Scientific and Cultural Organisation (UNESCO) began to function in 1946, a world-wide operation to eradicate illiteracy once and for all was in the forefront of its projected activities.

So far, I have written about 'illiteracy', or 'ability to read and write', without attempting to define these terms. They need definition, though this is not an easy matter. The point of reading and writing is to make communication possible. Communication is a two-way business. A person who can only read or only write (if indeed such a person exists) cannot, for any practical purpose, be described as 'literate'. Again, a person who has only learnt to sign his name, or to recognise his own name when he sees it written or printed, is at the barest minimum level of literacy. Statistics which count as illiterate only those who sign their names by making a mark may, in fact, be very misleading. Indeed, all statistical information on this subject is extremely difficult to assess, because different countries apply different minimum standards; and, whatever standard is adopted, the question whether particular individuals do or do not attain to it is not easy to answer without more detailed enquiry than a census enumerator is usually in a position to conduct.

Minimum literacy is not of much use except in so far as it may be developed into what is now termed 'functional literacy'. Obviously, no exact or universal definition of this term is possible, but its meaning is clear enough. 'A person is functionally literate', writes Professor William S. Gray, 'when he has acquired the knowledge and skills in reading and writing which enable him to engage effectively in all those activities in which literacy is normally assumed in his culture or group.'[8] He should at least be able to read a simple instruction leaflet in his own or some other familiar language, to write a legible letter, and to keep a record of his money transactions or the produce of his farm. This is the kind of literacy which matters and at which literacy campaigns are directed. If people below this functional level are classed as being, for practical purposes, illiterate, it is safe to say that the number of adult illiterates in the world substantially exceeds the accepted figure of 700 million and is more like 1,000 million. For this reason, some experts hold that, taking into account the enormous extent of the problem and the comparative paucity of the resources available, it is better to concentrate effort on the teaching of functional literacy to those who need it in order to fulfil adequately their place in the community, rather than to disperse effort in teaching minimum literacy to people who can, for the time being, continue to get on without it.

The question of language is more complicated than might appear at first sight. In some countries there is a single established language, and literacy will obviously be taught in that language. But in many of the countries in which illiteracy prevails there are dozens, sometimes even hundreds, of spoken languages so diverse that even neighbouring communities cannot communicate with each other; this did not, after all, matter when they had little or no opportunity or occasion for communication. Often, in such cases, there is a *lingua franca* which covers several local language areas, possibly the whole country. This may be a local tongue (such as Swahili), or an international language (such as English or French). The latter arrangement is frequently found in countries which have been or still are dependencies of a European power. The extent, however, to which the common language is used by the people at large as well as by the educated class may vary greatly from place to place.

One major difficulty is that information on language distribution and usage in many of these countries is very inadequate, and the subject is one on which a great deal of research remains to be done. But in any case there are several factors that have to be taken into consideration before, in any multi-lingual area, it is decided in which language or languages literacy is to be taught. I shall refer to these in Chapter 9. At this stage it is enough to note that the legacy of Babel adds a further dimension to the problem of illiteracy in many of the places where that problem is already most acute.

Another question is: how far is the teaching of literacy to be classed as 'education'? Traditionally, it has been so considered; administratively, it is frequently handled by education authorities. On the face of it, this seems reasonable and even inevitable, but there are arguments against as well as for the traditional system, as I hope to show.

A further general consideration which needs to be borne in mind is that the problem of illiteracy cannot be solved merely by teaching people to read. To read what? That is the question. There is no point in teaching literacy unless there are things for the literate to read when he has acquired the skill. A survey of the problem must, therefore, embrace the production and distribution of reading material.

In reviewing a global problem of this size, one is bound to use small-scale maps and talk in terms of percentages. It is easy to forget that underneath the statistics are human beings. 'For two-thirds of humanity the twentieth century does not exist', says a UNESCO publication. Yet it exists, though not for them. In the twentieth-century world the person who has not been given the chance to read is deprived of a fundamental human right. 'The illiterate' is a man, or woman, who is condemned to a status which, in the circumstances of today, is less than human. The illiterate is a man who, having scraped together ten shillings to meet the tax collector's demand, cheerfully walks away with a receipt showing that he has paid five shillings. The illiterate is a mother who has to trust someone else to read her letters from her absent son and send him her replies. The illiterate is a farmer who cannot decipher the simple instructions which could save his crop from disaster. The illiterate is a woman whose baby is dying of some malady which the poster on the wall tells how to prevent or cure. The illiterate is a man who goes on a train journey not knowing whether he has been charged the proper fare, not able to read the destination named on his ticket or the names of the stations through which he passes. The illiterate is an old woman crying because she envies her granddaughter who can go to school, a man who can only count by his fingers, a woman who told her teacher that she must learn to read as she was tired of getting on to the wrong bus.

It has been said that 'the illiterate and the reader of limited ability are everywhere the forgotten people of the world'.[9] But the world is waking up to remember them, and not too soon. It is nearly half a century since the Russian revolution took place, and over thirty years since, as will be told, an officially backed movement for eradicating illiteracy in a developing country was launched in the Philippine islands with the techniques first worked out by a missionary in order that men might read the Bible, and now adopted and adapted in literacy campaigns all over the world. Yet it is only in the present decade that a convergence of motives has forced the issue to the forefront of national and international policies. The original enthusiasm of the Christian missionaries has continued and intensified. It has been reinforced by the zeal of the humanitarian to help men to conquer poverty and disease by first conquering ignorance; by the economist's recognition that production and trade cannot expand so long as illiteracy handicaps the peoples of half the world; by the political thinker's realisation that peace and international understanding cannot be achieved while nations are divided within themselves and among one another by the unbridged gulf separating the literate from the illiterate.

I shall attempt to define the problem, its nature and its scope; to describe some of the efforts that have been made by voluntary bodies, by governments and by international organisations to find some solution; to indicate what in fact has to be done, and what methods and techniques have been devised in order to do it; and, in the light of all this, to consider what lessons have been learned, what measure of success has been achieved, and what prospects, if any, exist of dealing with the situation before it becomes too late for any effective action.

2

SOUND AND SYMBOL

No one can say how many spoken languages there are in the world. It depends upon how one defines a language, as distinct from a dialect, and on this authorities differ. Languages come and go, sometimes taking a long time to die. However, on a rough estimate, the number of currently spoken distinct languages is somewhere about 3,000.

Language is what distinguishes man from all other animals. Animals use sounds to communicate with each other in a general way: to announce the presence of danger or of food, the desire to mate, the warning off of an intruder. But man alone has invented the art of using articulated vocal sounds to denote particular objects and their location in time and space; and wherever man is, this art, in however rudimentary a form, is practised. Moreover, in practically all human societies now existing in the world, this art has been developed so that words originally associated with concrete objects are used metaphorically to express abstract thought.

A language, however defined, consists of a set of articulate vocal sounds which are conventionally accepted within a particular group of human beings as having particular meanings. There is no necessary connection between those meanings and the sound itself. A child makes itself understood by speaking of a 'bow-wow', but when we say 'dog' we are using a purely conventional symbol, the origin of which, according to the Oxford Dictionary, is not even known. The scientist can identify families of languages and trace them back to their primitive roots; but human communities, developing their own social organisations in isolation from one another, have built up their own conventions and idioms on ever-diverging lines, so that languages which spring from common roots become so different both in symbolism and in pronunciation as to be quite useless for the purpose of communication between the groups concerned.

The spoken word is universal in human society, but it exists only in time and has no permanence. The words once said and heard exist no more, except in the memory of the speaker and hearer. There is no record of them, no means—at any rate there has been none until the tape recorder was invented in modern times—of preserving them for the information and use of others. The organisation of a society in which the spoken word alone is used can be developed up to a point, but when it has reached the limit of the usefulness of oral tradition, reposing in the memories of the elders, it must become static. It may continue to serve the needs of the community so long as these also remain static; but the community is ill-equipped to meet with changes of circumstances and is at a great disadvantage in any external relations in which it may be involved, especially with peoples who have progressed to the use of the written and printed word.

In some remote dawn of history men discovered the art of making pictures of animals and objects. Originally these pictures were made for religious or magical purposes, but some communities hit on the idea of using them for making records. In the early Egyptian and Aztec civilisations, for example, forms of picture-writing were developed to a high degree of efficiency. The real breakthrough came, however, when some unknown genius introduced the practice of conventionalising these visual symbols so as to represent, not objects, but articulated sounds, and of combining them to signify the combinations of sounds which make up spoken words. 'It was', in the words of Professor R. A. Wilson, 'the most momentous and fruitful single achievement of the human intellect, since it was the condition of all the cumulative progress that man has since made in the world of free mind, which is his peculiar sphere.'[1]

The truth of this observation is shown by the different history of peoples who have adopted this system (generally known as the 'alphabet') and those, notably the Chinese, who developed their written language on the principle of using visual symbols to denote not sound but meaning. In practice, a limited number of symbols can supply all necessary needs. In the Polynesian languages, no more than twelve sound-symbols (letters) are required to reproduce all spoken words.[2] Even a language so rich in its varieties of pronunciation as English could (according to George Bernard Shaw) be reproduced by a phonetic alphabet of sixty-eight letters.[3] But the number of possible *meanings* is infinite. The Chinese classical language demands some 40–50,000 'characters', though the number of words with different sounds is only about 600. Inevitably, therefore, until modern movements were made towards the compilation of a Chinese phonetic alphabet, literacy in China was confined to a small percentage of the population, that is, those who had the ability and the facilities to undertake the enormous labour of memorising the large number of symbols. The cultural achievements of Chinese civilisation were very great indeed; but social and economic development could not progress beyond a certain point, and China found itself at a serious disadvantage when, in the nineteenth and twentieth centuries, it was obliged to confront the impact of the Western powers. Japan was in a better position, for a phonetic system had been in use there for at least a thousand years.

The alphabets established by other peoples—notably the Roman, Greek, Russian, Arabic and Sanskrit alphabets and their derivatives—are believed to stem from a common origin which is lost in the mists of antiquity. It appears that an alphabet was already in use about 1500 BC, and that it originated amongst the Semitic peoples.[4] As with the spoken word, different peoples developed independently their own techniques of fitting visual symbols to sounds. When all writing had to be done by hand, economy of effort was a consideration. Some scripts dispensed with vowels, all employed contractions and short cuts of various kinds. Alphabets devised to suit a particular spoken tongue were taken over by the speakers of other tongues and adapted to sounds for which they had not been designed. The so-called Roman alphabet, which today has the widest circulation of any, is in fact notoriously ill-adapted to the English spoken language. It contains three unnecessary consonants (Q, C and X), no symbols at all for some of the commonest consonantal sounds and five vowel symbols to represent at least eighteen distinct vowel sounds. The same difficulty applies, though usually in a less degree, to most modern languages. Russian is an exception. The Russian Cyrillic alphabet is derived, not from the Roman, but from the Greek. Before the Revolution it contained several unnecessary letters. 'When Lenin became dictator he abolished the unnecessary letters and made the Russian alphabet perfect. There is but one letter for a sound and one sound for a letter.'[5] Even so, the Russians encountered problems when it came to transcribing into the Cyrillic script the seventy or so separate languages spoken by the Asiatic peoples included in the Soviet Union.

Three thousand years were to elapse between the invention of the alphabet and the introduction of printing. This new development, which enormously increased the range and usefulness of the written word, was well served by a comparatively short and simple alphabet such as the Roman, but more complicated scripts such as the Arabic were ill-suited to the medium. In modern times, much ingenuity has gone to the revision and simplification of these scripts to enable them to be reproduced by the printing press and the typewriter. As Laubach observes, 'the adoption of a new alphabet is an exceedingly difficult, if not impossible, achievement in any country without the aid of a dictator.'[6] Turkey provides a notable instance of a complete change being successfully achieved. Mustapha Kemal, when he assumed the government, abolished the Arabic alphabet and made use of the Roman alphabet compulsory. By contrast, efforts in India to secure the general adoption of a uniform script have met with much difficulty. Still less success has attended well-intentioned plans to introduce an international phonetic alphabet suitable for all languages.

More will be said of these matters in later pages, when the progress of literacy programmes is being discussed. Here it suffices to make a passing reference to a purely practical factor in the use and spread of the written word, namely the matter of writing materials. Paper is such an essential and universal commodity today that a world without paper is almost inconceivable. The Babylonians scratched their records on bricks and tiles. The Peruvians worked out an elaborate system of using knotted cords. The Romans used wax-covered wooden tablets for casual notes and parchment made from animal membranes for more permanent memoranda. The Ten Commandments, if tradition be correct, were inscribed on slabs of stone, such as were in common use in the ancient world and are one of the principal sources of our archaeological knowledge. It is no doubt fortunate for the historian that the ancients were obliged to use such durable materials: but what made literacy and literature possible was the Egyptian invention of the papyrus: the thin skin of the riverside reeds, peeled and stuck together to make sheets which could be written upon, folded into flat books or rolled into scrolls. It was eventually superseded by the more efficient, cheap and readily available medium of paper. Paper —made by the pressure of wet vegetable pulp into flat sheets— was invented by the Chinese, and may rank as their greatest gift to civilisation. It reached Europe by way of the Arab world about AD 1200, and mass production by means of water mills was developed in time for the introduction of printing about AD 1450.[7]

Once the written word becomes established in any community as a general means of communication, and especially when printed matter begins to circulate, the visual symbol takes on a life of its own and, so far from becoming secondary or ancillary to the spoken word, assumes predominance. To anyone brought up in a literate community, a 'word' is thought of primarily as something written or printed rather than as a spoken sound. There may be variations in spelling, but these tend to be reduced as literacy spreads, and in any case they are negligible compared with the variations in accent and pronunciation which occur from time to time and place to place. The English language is particularly rich in illustrations of the way in which the written word, originating as a combination of sound-symbols, becomes eventually a symbol of meaning, though retaining enough of a visual, if not of an aural, link with its origin to escape the difficulties experienced by the Chinese. We find, for example, the English using the letter-combinations *sh* and *ti* to represent exactly the same spoken sound (as in *dash* and *ration*), according to whether the word in question is derived from a Teutonic or a Latin source. We find words of identical sound (such as *hare* and *hair*) having totally different meanings which can be distinguished only by the spelling: sometimes not even by that.

While, then, in first reducing a spoken language to writing, it may be a relatively simple matter of devising visual symbols to represent vowel and consonant sounds, this is only a beginning. The customary pronunciation of words will inevitably be modified as time goes on. Old words will take on new meanings as mental horizons widen with cultural development and terms originally denoting concrete objects and spatial relationships take on figurative significance. New words have to be invented, or more probably borrowed from other languages, to cover technical subjects for which the original language has no provisions; and the meaning of these words will be indicated by their visual appearance and not by their spoken sound, which may bear no resemblance at all to that of their sound in the language from which they have been derived.

These considerations imply a need for caution in approaching the very natural pressures that arise from time to time for adopting a simplified phonetic spelling in such languages as English. At a strictly utilitarian level, technology demands a vocabulary of terms with precise meanings; and these can be fully understood only by considering the shape and structure of the written word. Very largely, the words are borrowed or compounded from 'dead' languages, notably Latin and ancient Greek, which in fact we can only know in their visual form; we have never heard them spoken by those who devised them. To spell them phonetically according to some one of the many possible varieties of pronunciation would cause utter confusion and entirely destroy their value.

When I first learnt Latin at school, we pronounced it as if the words had been English. Caesar was Seezar, and his famous statement *Veni, vidi, vici*, was pronounced Veeneye, Veye-dye, Veye-sye. Then my school adopted the 'new' pronunciation, which was supposed to be more like that used by Caesar himself. He became Keyezar, and his statement Waynee, Weedee, Weekee. I went on to another school, and back to the 'old' pronunciation. Then this school also was converted to the 'new'. But it all made very little difference. It was always the same book and the same old Caesar writing the same old stuff about the Gallic wars.

It is not merely a matter of technical terms. The full life calls not only for basic literacy, not even only for 'functional' literacy, but for what we may perhaps venture to describe as 'cultural' literacy. Words have histories and associations. They carry overtones. They enshrine and communicate the wisdom of the sage, the inspiration of the prophet, the imagination of the poet. A people cannot be described as truly literate until it enjoys the capacity to produce and to appreciate *literature*. And literature, as its very name denotes, is a function of the written word. There were, doubtless, poets before Homer, but where are they now? Where would Christianity be without the Gospels, Islam without the Koran?

'I have built', wrote Horace, 'a memorial more enduring than bronze'. (*Exegi monumentum aere perennius*). He was right: but only because his memorial was in the written word. So let it be with Shakespeare. It is very probable that, if Burbage could have heard Sir John Gielgud reciting one of the soliloquies of Hamlet, he would scarcely have recognised it. We have, in fact, somewhat 'modernised' Shakespeare's spelling in the editions now current. It is questionable whether there has really been any advantage in this, for a modern reader would have no serious difficulty in understanding the original spelling. But at least we have not attempted to translate Shakespeare into modern English by daring to change his *words* where these have become obsolete or altered in meaning since his days.

Today there exist some 1,233 languages into which the whole or part of the Christian Bible—the most widely circulated book in the world—has been translated. It is probable that most of the languages which are used by a substantial number of people and adequately serve the needs of a community in the modern world have now been committed to writing and to print. Some may die out in time, but the very fact of their having been established in visual form gives them a degree of permanence which would not have been theirs as spoken tongues, and they may have future potentialities undreamed of today.

A good case could be made out for a theory that the great flowerings of literary genius have been associated with periods in which a language has become newly available to writers and readers and has been fertilised by being brought into touch, through the written word, with other cultures and tongues. The literary glory of classical Greece began with the circulation in written form of the ballads sung by Homer and his predecessors, and was developed in a time of continuous if uneasy contact with the arts and cultures of Persia and of Egypt. Greece, in her turn, as Horace confessed, made captive by Rome made her rough conqueror captive. The glories of the Augustan age of Latin literature are amongst the great masterpieces of the writer's art. Till then the written language had been used mainly for the purpose of recording laws and official appointments. Vergil, Horace, Cicero, Ovid, Terence, Livy and others took over the ideas, the literary forms, the imagery and often the words of the Greek authors and made something new and distinctive of their own.

So, too, it was with the Elizabethan age in England. The fusion of Saxon and Norman was still a new thing, and the written English language was but recently crystallised by the introduction of printing and the wide circulation and unique authority of the English Bible in its earlier translations which preceded and led up to King James's version of 1611. When Shakespeare wrote down his plays, the language was still developing and continually being enriched by the new learning of the Renaissance. It was a period of excitement and exuberant experiment in deploying the magic of words. Shakespeare's great genius was matched to the hour. At another time, in another place, he might have made no mark.

Who knows how many Vergils and Shakespeares, Newtons and Einsteins, may await the opportunities which literacy alone can make available? Literacy campaigns are usually thought of as purely practical efforts to enable the people concerned to improve their agriculture, hygiene and business. It is perhaps even more important to consider the potential contribution of literacy to the enlargement of the minds of men and to the sum of human achievement in the world of the imagination and the spirit.

3

THE MAP OF ILLITERACY

NO COUNTRY or community can claim to have a population which is permanently and completely literate. Leaving infants aside, there are always, even in the most sophisticated and highly organised societies, the odd individuals who, on account of mental deficiency or some exceptional deprivation of opportunity, have never learned or, if they have learned, have forgotten how to read and write. In 'advanced' societies illiteracy, as such, does not constitute a problem and they can be left out of account for the purpose of the present discussion. In the statistics of illiteracy published by UNESCO in 1965 it was decided to exclude 'countries or territories in which the illiteracy rate among the population aged fifteen and over was estimated at less than 5 per cent in the last census or literacy survey. This particularly applies to most European countries, the USSR, the USA, Canada, Australia, New Zealand, Japan, Argentine and Cuba.'[1]

Percentages, however, always a tricky business, are never more so than in this matter of illiteracy. They may fairly be accepted as guides at the extreme ends of the scale. If we exclude from consideration countries with less than 5 per cent of illiteracy, we may reasonably regard countries with more than, say, 50 per cent as having a problem of illiteracy on their hands; and the higher the percentage the more serious and intractable the problem is likely to be. Looked at from another point of view, we may fairly say that, irrespective of percentages, any government which has more than 5 million adult illiterates in its popu-

24

lation has an illiteracy problem. Such governments include those of Afghanistan, Brazil, China, Egypt, Ethiopia, India, Indonesia, Iran, Korea, Nigeria, Pakistan, Tanzania, Turkey and the Republic of Vietnam.

From a statistical point of view, the selection of 'countries or territories' as the units for consideration is no doubt very unsatisfactory. Countries vary greatly in size and in population. The criteria adopted by different governments for estimating the extent of illiteracy also vary widely; so does the expertness of the census-takers who have to apply the criteria. A given percentage of illiteracy as stated in the records may mean one thing in one country and something rather different in another. The larger the country concerned, the less reliable the national figure may be as indicating the presence or absence of a problem of illiteracy. As the UNESCO document already referred to points out, a national average may conceal the existence of definite social groups perhaps contained within specific areas. For example, it might be found on examination that in a particular country with an apparently low illiteracy rate, the literates were in fact mainly concentrated in one or more urban centres, while the rural populations were almost completely illiterate.

Nevertheless, from a practical point of view, the question has to be considered in terms of 'countries or territories'—in other words, areas controlled by separate governments. Today most of these separate governments are internationally recognised as of sovereign status, but there remain a few which are dependent on one or other of the major powers, yet are distinct and identifiable geographical and administrative entities. Wherever a problem of illiteracy exists, it is the government responsible for that place which has to deal with it, whether on its own account or with help from outside as it, and it alone, may decide. While, therefore, a breakdown of illiteracy statistics according to geographical regions, races, religions or other possible divisions, may be valuable for particular purposes, what one really needs to know is which governments have an illiteracy problem on their hands and what is being or can be done about it by that government.

The basic material for studying the distribution of illiteracy is contained in the UNESCO publication *World Illiteracy at Mid-Century*, a statistical survey published in 1957. This embodies the results of earlier official and unofficial studies and gives as complete a picture as was practicable of the situation in every country of the world round about 1950. It was supplemented in 1965 by a document, *Statistics of Illiteracy*, prepared by UNESCO for the World Congress of Ministers of Education on the Eradication of Illiteracy which was held at Teheran in September of that year. This is necessarily a less complete survey than that of 1957, but it provides information, broken down into age-groups and sexes, of the position reached in 1962 in most of the countries in which illiteracy constitutes a problem.

Taking the world as a whole, the accepted figure, as was observed in the first chapter of this book, for the number of adult illiterates existing in 1950 is about 700 million, representing between 40 and 45 per cent of the world's adult population at that time. But, 'taking the large number of semi-illiterates into account, people are saying with increasing frequency (at international meetings, in scientific circles, in many books and periodicals, etc.) that our world is "a world of a thousand million illiterates" '.[2] Comparison of the 1962 figures with those of 1950 shows that, while in the interval the *percentage* of illiterates in the world population had slightly diminished, from 40–45 to 38–43, the *absolute* number of adult illiterates had actually increased with the growth of the world population. There were, in UNESCO's member states, nearly 35 million more illiterates in 1962 than in 1950, despite all the work that had been done by national and international effort to deal with the problem during those twelve years. A breakdown of the illiteracy figures by continental areas gives the following results, which are based on a large number of assumptions and cannot, therefore, be regarded as fully reliable; but they are acceptable as a rough guide.

ILLITERACY PERCENTAGES BY CONTINENTAL AREAS[3]

	1950	1962
Africa	80–85	78–84
America, North and South	20–21	18–20
Arab countries	82–87	78–82
Asia and Oceania	67–71	53–57
Europe and Soviet Union	6–10	3– 7

Such a table is of some value as showing where most of the major areas of illiteracy will be found, but clearly further analysis is necessary. Europe cannot, as such figures would suggest, be entirely ruled out of account as an area where there are no illiteracy problems. It is, however, fair to say that, where relatively high percentages exist—as, for example, in Portugal, Greece, Yugoslavia, Bulgaria, Rumania, Malta—they may be considered as indicating short-term rather than long-term problems, which can and doubtless will be dealt with by expansion and improvement of existing machinery for child and adult education in the countries concerned.

The figure for the American continent, again, is an average which is brought down by the very low illiteracy rate of that half of the population which lives in the United States and Canada. In fact, some of the countries of Central and South America and the Caribbean are among those in which the most serious problems of illiteracy are present. In Asia, on the other hand, Japan and Israel are almost alone in showing anything like a low proportion of illiterates, while in Africa there is no country (leaving aside the little island of St Helena) in which less than half the adult population were classed in 1950 as illiterate, and in most of the countries the illiteracy percentage was anything from 75 to 99. The 1962 figures did not indicate any significant change in this general picture.

Passing from percentages to numbers, the official estimate of the position in 1962 was that, in the age-group fifteen to forty-four, which covers the most active section of the population, there were 94 million illiterates in Africa, 243 million in Asia, 34 million in America, and 9 million in Europe.[4]

A map of illiteracy would, therefore, show the black spots mainly grouped in certain well-defined areas: the whole of Africa; the whole of Asia (excluding the Soviet Union), with a few exceptions in relatively small geographical areas, notably Japan; the islands of the Pacific, again with a few exceptions; Central and Southern America and the Caribbean, excepting Argentina, Uruguay, the Panama Canal Zone, and some of the islands, and with a question mark concerning some other islands and some of the smaller republics. Each of these large areas includes countries differing widely in size, constitution, natural resources and historical background. To make out a complete list here would be tedious for the reader and would merely reproduce the information available in the UNESCO documents already referred to. There may, however, be some advantage in taking a brief look at each region and noting some of the salient points.

The heading 'Africa' covers some fifty or more separate administrative units, ranging in size from Egypt and Nigeria, with populations of well over 20 million each and formidable illiteracy figures, to the island of St Helena with a population of 5,000 and no adult illiteracy. North and east of the Sahara desert are the African Arab states—Morocco, Algeria, Tunisia, Libya, Sudan, Egypt—whose long history of contact with oriental and occidental cultures has yet not saved them from having very high illiteracy rates. South of the Zambesi are South Africa and Rhodesia, with their special racial problems; South-West Africa; part of Mozambique, subject to the government of Portugal; and Lesotho (Basutoland), Botswana (Bechuanaland) and Swaziland, former British territories just emerging to independence. Off the coast is the great island of Madagascar, formerly part of the French colonial empire. If this were not diversity enough, there are the countries in the great land mass stretching from the Sahara to the Zambesi. It includes the ancient empire of Ethiopia; the old-established independent state of Liberia; the newly enfranchised countries which ten years ago were ruled by Britain, France and Belgium; and Angola still ruled by Portugal. Here are some twenty governments, all of which face an enormous and baffling problem of illiteracy.

The Asian picture is no less complex. The Chinese People's Republic contains at least 600 million people. Detailed information about the régime's efforts to overcome illiteracy is scanty, but there can be no doubt that great strides have been made in recent years. The prominence given to the writings of Chairman Mao Tse-tung in the 'cultural revolution' of 1966–67 presupposes that these writings can be read by a wide public. Thirty million copies are said to have been produced for circulation in this connection. Posters and wall newspapers appear in profusion in streets and factories. Kurt Mendelssohn, who visited China in September 1966, found evidence of 'a new high degree of literacy'.[5] While, therefore, the estimated rate of illiteracy at mid-century was 50 per cent, it may well now be considerably less. India and Pakistan contain another 500 million or more people and have serious problems of illiteracy which they are striving to tackle by national effort. Ceylon, Burma, Malaysia and Indonesia all face the problem in varying degrees. So do the Arab states, Iran, Turkey, Thailand and Korea. In all, Asia is held to be the home of three-quarters of the world's illiterates. The islands of the Pacific cannot offer anything to compare with these numbers, but they comprise some twenty separate administrative units, ranging in population from a million or so (New Guinea and the British Solomon Islands) to one or two thousand, and in almost all the percentage of illiteracy is high. The kingdom of Tonga is an honourable exception.

The countries of Central and South America show sharp contrasts. To some extent these are connected with the racial composition of the populations. Where a large proportion of the people is of European or part-European descent, the rate of illiteracy tends to be lower than where the majority is of indigenous origin. Thus, in Ecuador, where the illiteracy rate for the whole country is estimated at between 40 and 50 per cent, the rate for the Indian group (nearly a third of the population) is as much as 90 per cent.[6] These countries have, however, one advantage over those of Africa and Asia in that the Spanish and Portuguese languages cover the great part of the subcontinent, though some of the Indian vernaculars are still very much alive. Of the Caribbean islands it may be said that—apart from Cuba, which is not now classed as an 'area of illiteracy', and Haiti, where the illiteracy percentage is something like 90 per cent and where 85 per cent of the population speak a language not yet reduced to writing[7]—the average percentage is now round about 25 per cent, variations again being due to differences of history, racial composition and geographical situation. Generally speaking, there has been steady progress in the Caribbean area during the last half-century in reducing the rate of illiteracy by the development of educational services, more particularly for girls. In the Jamaican census of 1943, the female rate was actually lower than the male, which is an unusual situation.[8]

4

PIONEER ATTACKS ON ILLITERACY

THE IDEA of systematically teaching adults to read and write, as distinct from teaching children as an essential part of their basic education, is comparatively modern. The campaigns and programmes with which most of this book will be concerned have taken place in the present century and under official auspices, with the motive of improving the social, cultural and economic life of the peoples in question.

The main credit for the earliest efforts to develop adult literacy must go to the Christian churches, and more particularly to those of the Protestant persuasion. Until the time of the Reformation, Catholic as well as Orthodox Christianity rested its claims on two pillars: the Scriptures and the tradition of the Church. The formulation and definition of doctrine were matters for the authorities of the Church, guided by the Holy Spirit, and embodied in decisions promulgated by a General Council of the whole Church—for example, the Council of Nicaea held in AD 325—or (in Western Christendom) by the Bishop of Rome. The Scriptures were the basic documents, and no doctrine could be taught that was not consistent with them; but tradition might justify the teaching of doctrine which was not in fact to be found in the Scriptures themselves.

Whatever view may be taken for or against this position, the Christians who broke away from the Roman obedience in the sixteenth century were left with the Scriptures as the one infallible authority. The leaders of the Reformation movements naturally took steps to have the Bible translated into the languages spoken by the people and to teach the people to read in order that they might search the Scriptures for themselves. In England and Wales, in the eighteenth century, the churches founded Sunday Schools to help the general population of the country to read, and it is largely due to such Christian efforts that these countries reached a high degree of literacy at a comparatively early date.

The pattern has been repeated overseas. As early as 1714, a printing press provided by the Society for Promoting Christian Knowledge produced at Tranquebar in South India the first book in the Tamil language: a translation of the Gospels and the Acts of the Apostles. When the pioneer British missionary William Carey went to India in the eighteenth century, one of his first preoccupations was to translate the Bible into local languages and teach the people to read it. In Asia, Africa and throughout the 'mission field', it was the Christian and especially the Protestant churches which laid the foundations of education and of literacy. 'For churches the first great motive in teaching illiterates is to enable them to read the Bible. Literacy and Bible translation are twins. Perhaps it would be better to call them the two legs on which the Bible must walk into every mind and heart on earth.'[1]

In 1804, the British and Foreign Bible Society began its mammoth task of providing in due course the Christian Bible for every man in his own tongue at a price which he could afford. Other Bible societies were formed in Europe and North America to take part in this enterprise. The basic work was done by missionaries in the field, and the results co-ordinated, edited and prepared for publication by the expert headquarters staffs of the societies. In very many cases, the translators had to begin by reducing an unwritten language to visual symbols. This was a formidable task, and there was necessarily much trial and error in the initial stages. Many languages contain sounds that do not exist in any European tongue and for which the normal alphabets provide no suitable symbol. And in any case, as already noted, the same symbols are made to do duty for very many different sounds in the various European languages. Intensive research has been going on for many years and the science of phonetics is far advanced, but there are still many languages that have not been fully studied. A large number have no recognised alphabet; some have alphabets which are seriously imperfect; others have two or more rival alphabets in use.

In India, China, Africa and the Pacific, the modern impetus towards the conquest of illiteracy was begun and developed by the missionaries, primarily in order that people might read the Bible. The idea of literacy's being actively promoted by the state as a public service in the interests of social development is of comparatively recent growth. The earliest wholly successful national effort to promote literacy was that of Japan. Until the middle of the nineteenth century, Japan's main cultural contacts were with China; and, although the Japanese had had a phonetic system (based on syllables) for at least a thousand years, it was supplemented by the use of large numbers of Chinese characters—hence it was not easily used by the ordinary people. When direct contact with the West was established in 1853, Japan rapidly picked up what the Westerners had to offer in the way of knowledge, techniques and experience. Compulsory education was introduced in 1872—nearly as early as in Britain—and by 1900 illiteracy had virtually disappeared. By contrast, in China, the progress of literacy was hampered by the difficulty of the written language. Although several ideas were tried out by the missionaries, little real advance was made until, during and immediately after the First World War, a literacy movement initiated by the Young Men's Christian Association was taken up and developed on a national basis. Even then progress was slow until very recent times.

Soviet Union

In Russia under the Czars, it was held that to teach the general mass of the people to read would do more harm than good; but it is Russia which provides the most outstanding example of effective government action to eradicate illiteracy. A considerable amount of detailed information has recently been made available in a series of reports prepared by the USSR Commission for UNESCO in connection with a seminar for African planners and organisers of adult literacy programmes held at Tashkent in 1965. Most of what follows is based upon these documents.

In 1897, only a quarter of the population in Russia could read and write. Of the peasantry, 93 per cent were illiterate. Among the non-Russian Asiatic peoples the illiteracy rate was even higher. Many of the communities had not even an alphabet. Lenin put the conquest of illiteracy at the head of the reforms judged necessary in order to build up a socialist society. 'An illiterate man', he said, 'is non-political; first he must be taught to read.' In 1919 he signed a decree laying down that 'the entire population of the republic aged from eight to fifty years who cannot read and write are obliged to learn to do so either in their native or in the Russian language according to their choice'.[2] In July 1920, an All-Russia Special Commission for the Elimination of Illiteracy was set up to organise the provision of teaching institutions, the training of teachers, the working out of teaching methods and the production of textbooks. It had power to compel literate people to teach the others and to bring criminal proceedings against anyone who refused to fulfil this duty or to hamper the policy. From 1923, the official campaign was supplemented by the activities of a voluntary society called 'Down with Illiteracy', of the Young Communist League and of many other organisations.

One of the reports referred to gives a graphic description of the campaign:

A great number of streamers and posters on the elimination of illiteracy was circulated all over the country. Here are some of the most popular slogans of the time: 'Down with Illiteracy!' 'Illiteracy goes hand in hand with ruin!' 'Literacy is a sword that will smash the Forces of Darkness', 'It is the right and duty of every citizen to be literate', 'Literacy is the road to Communism!'

. . . People learned everywhere: at schools, at clubs, in the barracks, in the offices, in the open air. And civilians were not the only ones to learn . . . elimination of illiteracy became compulsory for the whole army. In some military detachments illiterate service-men were grouped into separate companies and battalions. People struggled with their letters whenever they could: between operations in the trenches, on guard or on detail duty. Every kind of printed matter was used as textbooks—newspapers, home-made alphabets, posters, booklets.

. . . Everywhere throughout the country a wide network of anti-illiteracy centres was being set up. They were opened wherever illiterate people were to be found, at club rooms of factories, plants and mines, at the living quarters of the workers, in kitchens of apartments shared by several families, at clubs, libraries and village reading rooms. . . . Illiterate women burdened with children received instruction at home if they could not attend classes.[3]

The government was, of course, in a singularly favourable position to conduct such a campaign, since it had complete power both to decree the elimination of illiteracy and to enforce its decision. It is hardly conceivable that this vast campaign could have been successfully conducted without some cutting back of the development of other highly desirable social services and public works, but the government was able to determine its own priorities. Fines, loss of job, and various other penalties were prescribed for people who failed to learn to read, but, states one of the Russian reports, 'the compulsion was of a moral character, no compulsion was necessary in practice. The entire work in teaching the illiterate people was based on persuasion.'[4] It seems, indeed, that the people generally responded with patriotic fervour, though there was some reluctance amongst the rural population, especially the women.

The huge scale of the campaign necessitated the recruitment of a 'cultural army' of volunteer instructors, most of whom had no teaching experience and went into action after attending short improvised courses. As a result there were admittedly some shortcomings in the early years. The instruction given by the barely trained volunteers was too sketchy and the pupils tended to relapse afterwards into illiteracy. However, from 1929 onwards, a better organised 'cultural offensive' was brought into effect. According to the official figures, over 2 million people were taught literacy in 1928–29, 8 million in 1929–30 and 11 million in 1930–31. By 1934, over 40 million adults had been made literate. At about the same time, primary education—which had been free since 1922—was made compulsory for all children. Continuing education for the adult literates and semi-literates was also organised.

The non-Russian-speaking states in the Soviet Union presented special difficulties. Some seventy languages are spoken in these countries, and in some of these languages there are numerous distinct dialects. About forty of the languages had never been reduced to writing at all. Educational facilities were practically non-existent. In some of the more remote areas the populations are nomadic, and the teachers had to travel along with their pupils, accompanying them to the hunting grounds for fur animals and the breeding-grounds for deer and reindeer. Much intensive and expert work was done to devise suitable alphabets for this multitude of languages. At first the Latin alphabet was taken as a basis, but at the end of the 1930s the Russian alphabet was adopted for all except a small number of states: the Georgians and Armenians preserved their own ancient alphabets, and the states in the Baltic area continued to base theirs on the Latin script. Special departments and publishing houses were set up to produce textbooks and other literature in the native languages.

By the end of 1939—twenty years from the start of the campaign—it was possible for the government to claim that, but for a small category of elderly peasant and working women, illiteracy had been virtually eradicated in the Soviet Union. Lenin's decree had been in the main fulfilled. By any standards this concentrated effort of a great nation must rank highly in the record of man's achievements as a social animal. Certainly, in the field now under discussion nothing comparable has yet taken place.

TURKEY

A less spectacular though notable success story can, however, be related of Turkey, defeated and shorn of its empire in the First World War. In 1923, the monarchy was displaced by a republican government and Mustapha Kemal took over. He found that only 10 per cent of the population was literate. The Turkish language was written in Arabic characters, though these did not fit it satisfactorily. In 1928, he effected a complete reorganisation. The Arabic alphabet was abolished at one stroke and the Roman alphabet adopted for all purposes. Free primary education was made compulsory, all old textbooks were scrapped and replaced by new ones, and everyone between the ages of sixteen and forty was required to become literate in the new alphabet. The president himself and thousands of volunteers taught in the 'folk schools', which, during the next seven years, were attended by $2\frac{1}{2}$ million men and women. By 1935, the adult illiteracy rate had dropped from 90 per cent to an average of 80 per cent (men about 70 per cent, women about 90 per cent), and by 1950 to an average of 68 per cent (men 52 per cent, women 83 per cent). By 1960, the percentages for males and females respectively over the age of ten were 43 and 75.

PHILIPPINES

The scene now shifts far across the world to the Philippine islands under the American flag, and there appears on the stage one who is justly celebrated as 'the father of literacy', Dr Frank

C. Laubach. I have already quoted more than once from the authoritative works in which he has recorded his unrivalled experience for the benefit of those engaged in literacy teaching, and I shall have many more occasions for doing so.

Born in 1882 in Benton, Pennsylvania, Frank Charles Laubach (he is PH.D. of Columbia University) was in due time ordained as a minister of the Congregational Church, and after his marriage in 1912 made up his mind to go as a missionary to the Philippines. These islands came under United States control after the Spanish-American war of 1898. Traditionally opposed in principle to 'colonialism', the Americans attached great importance to promoting the education of the island peoples, with a view to their eventually becoming independent. Large numbers of teachers were recruited and sent out by the United States government and also by the missionary bodies. Dr Laubach arrived in the islands in 1915, having been assigned by the American Board of Commissioners for Foreign Missions to general pastoral duties amongst the Moro people of Mindanao. In a book published thirty years later, he has left a graphic description, based on his letters written at the time, of the steps by which he was led to initiate a literacy campaign, 'although this was the farthest thing in the world from our intentions'.[5] It was not until 1929 that he was in a position to begin, when the turbulent Moros of Lanao, who had strongly resisted the American government, had been pacified. With a Filipino colleague, Donato Galia, Laubach set himself to learn the Maranaw language and reduce it to writing. A printing press was acquired, and a rudimentary newspaper was prepared for circulation.

The campaign at Lanao quickly gained momentum. It attracted interest in other parts of the Philippines and the cooperation of goverment authorities, Roman Catholic as well as Protestant missionaries and, indeed, of the Muslim leaders. It was extended to cover no less than twenty-one local languages. The Governor-General, Theodore Roosevelt Jr., was impressed and encouraged the development of literacy work under missionary auspices throughout the islands until the time was ripe for the government itself to take over. This point was reached in 1936. 'Thereafter', says Laubach, 'the literacy campaign became a government enterprise and reached out to every province and village. Literacy wagons were sent over the islands to attract all the illiterate adults and give them reading lessons. Adult night schools were established nearly everywhere.'[6] The prisons, it was said, were becoming universities, and the army was nearly 100 per cent literate when the war with Japan broke out.

His experience of creating a literacy campaign in the Philippines convinced Laubach that the techniques which had been worked out there—and especially the approach to the problem of teaching adults which the missionaries had developed—could be applied in principle to the conquest of illiteracy in other countries. In 1935, he visited Malaya, India, Egypt, Palestine, Syria and Turkey. In each place he made contact with the missionaries and others who were interested in literacy work, discussed their problems and gave advice. During this progress he helped to construct literacy charts in thirty languages. His growing reputation as an expert brought him requests from many quarters for his help and counsel. I shall refer later to his notable pioneer work in India. Here I will note that in 1937 he paid a brief visit to East Africa where, in Kenya, Zanzibar and Tanganyika, he found government departments and missionaries eager to take advantage of the advice which he could give them. He for his part, in dealing with African languages, discovered methods of improving upon the teaching techniques which had been worked out in Asian contexts, so that the benefit of these discussions was mutual.

In 1941, when the Japanese attacked Pearl Harbor, Laubach was on furlough in the United States. Unable to resume his work in Asia, he turned his attention to Latin America. Here, as elsewhere, literacy work had to a large extent been initiated by the evangelical missionaries, but by this time the movement had attracted official and public support. In his war-time tours,

Laubach helped the local people in most of the republics of Central and South America and in some of the principal islands to prepare literacy courses and to apply the teaching methods which had proved their value in Asia and Africa. 'One advantage', he commented, 'of making experiments in so many countries is that we can profit by mistakes and successes alike.'[7]

This is perhaps the convenient place in which to record that Dr Laubach continued to carry on literacy work in many parts of the world under the auspices of the Committee on World Literacy and Christian Literature (which in 1943 took the place of the previous American Committee) until he reached retirement age in 1955. He then formed an independent organisation, the Laubach Literacy Fund, Inc., in which, along with his son, Dr Robert S. Laubach, he continues to encourage and assist research and action 'helping to draw back the dark curtain of illiteracy'. In this work the University of Syracuse, N.Y., has played an important part.

Literacy campaigns cost money. One of the chief difficulties in the early efforts was lack of finance. The idea that the wealthier nations should help the poorer, through multilateral or bilateral assistance schemes, is of very modern growth. In the period before the Second World War, countries striving for social development had to find the money from their own resources or from charitable funds, or else go without. Where local resources were inadequate, only a powerful and indeed ruthless government could decide to allocate them to teaching literacy at the expense of other crying needs. It can be soundly argued that to do so is a good investment, since the first step towards a long-term solution of the problems of poverty and disease is to deal with the problem of ignorance. It is difficult, however, in a country where large numbers of the people have not enough to eat and are riddled with disease, to decree that the present generation must be content to starve and die in order that future generations may enjoy a better standard of living.

INDIA

India in the 1930s was estimated to contain 325 million illiterates—one-third of the illiterate population of the world. 'The idea', writes Dr Laubach, 'of teaching adults to read after they had passed out of school (age?) was not given serious consideration in India until this century.'[8] Indeed, during the first twenty years of the century, only a few small and isolated efforts were made. In the Punjab, for instance, a literacy campaign was started in 1921, but after achieving some initial success it faded away. In its vast scale and in the complexity of the linguistic and social background, the problem in India may be considered as comparable to that of the Soviet Union. India, however, lacked the two keys to success which the Soviets possessed: an authoritarian central government determined to give literacy the necessary priority and to use its powers, if need be, to make learning compulsory; and a national spirit dedicated to a militant justification of its independence and fed by an ideological doctrine passionately believed and insistently proclaimed.

In the 1930s, owing largely to the initiative and labours of Christian missionaries, illiteracy began to be seriously tackled in various parts of the subcontinent. The National Christian Council of India successfully appealed for help to the World Literacy Committee of the American missions, and arrangements were made for Dr Laubach, who had already visited India briefly, to make an extensive tour of the country in 1936–37. In the course of this journey he met Nehru, who warmly commended the literacy movement and encouraged him to press on. Gandhi, who had at an earlier stage confessed to doubts about the advisability of teaching Indians to read (because of the pernicious nature of much of the literature that reached the country from the West), was now thoroughly in support of the movement, and the Congress party, on taking office in 1938, made the teaching of literacy a prime object of policy. The basic idea of the campaigns undertaken at this stage was that people who could read, or who had been taught to read, should pass on their knowledge to their illiterate neighbours. 'Each one teach one' was the slogan. In several places people who were not willing or able to teach were invited instead to pay a contribution to the cost of the campaign, for money was still a major difficulty. In Bombay city, for instance, a campaign was sponsored in 1939 by an unofficial committee. It was estimated to cost only the modest sum of Rs 15,000, but the government could only put up Rs 3,000, leaving the balance to be provided by public-spirited citizens. One particularly successful effort was that made by the government of Bihar Province where, between May 1938 and June 1939, over 700,000 people were taught to read. In the United Provinces and other provinces and states, campaigns were organised with varying degrees of success. As a result, taking the country as a whole, there was an appreciable diminution of the illiteracy rate in terms of percentage.

Much of the above information is derived from the book in which Dr Laubach, to whose inspiration and advice these campaigns owed so much, summed up his observations, his counsels and his hopes. Writing in 1940, he considered that all the conditions for a 'stupendous advance' in India were then ready, or nearly ready, if only the general public could be mobilised. But this was precisely the difficulty. The war did not help matters, nor did the disturbed political conditions of the time. Real progress had to wait until after 1947, when India became a sovereign state. Intensive efforts to combat illiteracy were then set on foot by the government in both urban and rural areas, and considerable successes were recorded, despite some lack of central co-ordination and the slow response of some of the country folk. By 1951, the percentage of adult illiterates in the population had fallen to 80, as compared with 90 in 1931, but that meant that some 170 million people still could not read or write. By 1961, the figure had fallen further to 76 per cent, but the population had grown at such a rate that, although this meant that there were far more literate people in India than ever before, there were also well over 200 million illiterates.

5

MID-CENTURY EXPERIMENTS

INDIA was at no time part of the British colonial system. The British colonies and protectorates contained many areas of illiteracy, and although British colonial policy was at least as enlightened as that of any other power, it was generally accepted that these dependencies should be content to make such social progress as could be financed from local resources. Assistance from the mother country was mainly limited to technical advice which, between the wars, was forthcoming on an increasingly generous scale. Largely due to pressure from religious and philanthropic bodies, considerable attention was given in the Colonial Office to the encouragement of schemes for mass education and community development presented by colonial administrations, and the services of highly qualified experts were placed at the disposal of the Colonial Office and the territorial governments through a system of advisory committees. The eradication of illiteracy naturally had a part in such schemes, but few large-scale projects with this particular aim in view could be put into effect.

The general position was radically altered for the better by the British Parliament's passing, in 1940, the first of what was to be a long series of Colonial Development and Welfare Acts. Under these Acts, it became possible to allocate sums of money on a really significant scale for financing social as well as economic development in the colonial territories. Though shortage of manpower and technical apparatus made progress slow during the course of the war, plans were made and foundations laid so that swift and effective action could be taken when hostilities came to an end in 1945.

Since space does not allow detailed consideration of the many efforts made to deal with the problem of illiteracy in British colonial dependencies in the post-war years, those in Northern Nigeria, the Gold Coast (now Ghana) and Uganda have been chosen for examination here, mainly because information concerning them was readily accessible. These Commonwealth efforts should be studied in conjunction with the attempts to conquer illiteracy in French-speaking Africa and with the large-scale campaign put in operation in Cuba, which will also be considered in this chapter.

NORTHERN NIGERIA

The campaign conducted in Northern Nigeria in the 1950s is of special interest. Nigeria, which in 1960 became an independent federal republic, was the largest and most populous of the British territories in West Africa. The northern (inland) part of the country has a different historical and cultural background from the southern, coastal area. Until 1914, this northern part was a separate protectorate, but thereafter, until 1947, the whole country was brought under one British governor-general, the 'Northern Provinces' being administered by a lieutenant-governor responsible to him. After 1947, this area became the 'Northern Region'.

Under whatever name, this northern part of Nigeria has several marked characteristics distinguishing it from the south. The peoples of this area, who numbered some 17 to 20 million in the 1940s, are predominantly Muslim in religion(though there are considerable numbers of 'pagans' and some Christians), and their culture is largely linked with that of the Muslim world. The Hausa language is widely, though not universally, used. During the period of British administration, the government remained in the hands of territorial rulers—emirs and sultans—

who were provided with British advisers and technical experts under the system known as 'indirect rule'. Though comprising well over half of Nigeria in area and population, the Northern Region was at a disadvantage in comparison with the southern part of the country in adapting itself to twentieth-century needs. Historically, it had been isolated until this century from contact with Europe, whereas the peoples of the coast had had long and fruitful connections with the outer world. But, with the breakdown of that isolation due to modern development of communications and the need of other countries for the agricultural and mineral products of the land, the north could no longer afford to be in a 'backward' condition. One of the first necessities was to deal with the problem of illiteracy.

The genesis of the Northern Nigerian literacy campaign was thus described in 1955 by a distinguished African who played a leading part in it, Mallam Ahmadu Coomassie:

The Adult Education work started in 1946 when the Government of Nigeria seconded one Education Officer to organise and supervise the literacy classes that had sprung up in some of the keen areas of the country. The Campaign began as an Adult Literacy Campaign. People became eager to learn to read and write not so much for their value in their daily lives but because they were proud to be classified among the literate members of the communities. Classes sprang up like mushrooms. There were some interesting revelations about these classes. There was a case where some youths in a village formed their own society and made a rule that no one, who was illiterate, could be admitted into the society. There was another case of women in a small village who, having seen a neighbouring village properly laid out with communal roads leading to the village, threatened to leave their husbands unless they should attend a literacy class and become 'qualified' for a better laid out village. For, that was what they were told, that wherever they saw a well laid out village it was because people in the village were literate! In fact literacy became one of the three virtues to be possessed in a certain village: these virtues were BICYCLE, LITERACY, WIFE. There had been many such cases of

45

interesting stories during the early stage of the Campaign in the North.

The instructors were drawn from the local authority officials: they comprised school teachers, dispensers, scribes, district and village heads, etc. Most of them had had no training at all in the teaching method. This went on for about 4 years and then it was decided that, because of the number of classes that had been spreading about, each of the three Regions should have its own Officer, who would be in charge of the Adult Education Work.

The North Regional Adult Education Officer was selected from among the cadre of Education Officers. He has had a very long and wide experience of the country and the people. When he started his work, in 1950, it was agreed that only pilot schemes were to be sponsored by the Regional Government.

And then in 1952 the Regional Government decided to embark on a more comprehensive Adult Education Scheme. The census figures for 1952 show that the Region has a population of about 17,000,000. Of these only about 250,000 are literate in Roman script, that is less than 2 persons in a hundred. Of course 5·4 per cent more are literate in Arabic script; that brings the total percentage of literate to about 7·5. The rest, 92·5 per cent, are illiterate. This is not only disturbing, but it shows that the masses of the people have not the means and the opportunity to participate in the government of their country.

A Committee, known as 'Fighting Against Ignorance Committee', was formed in 1952, with the following terms of reference:

> To consider by what means, with the least delay, the people throughout the Region can be assisted to appreciate the circumstances under which they live today, and the ways by which it is the desire and policy of Government to improve their way of life, and to teach them politically, socially and economically to meet the future.

The establishment of the Committee was given wide publicity in the Region, and memoranda were invited from various persons, official and non-official, who are qualified by their experience and interest to advise on practical proposals for the conduct and organisation of a 'Campaign Against Ignorance'. As a result of their meetings and deliberations the Committee submitted 17 Recommendations which have since formed the basis of the Region-wide Campaign. These Recommendations included various forms of adult education work, and covered the following:

> Literacy Campaign; provision of reading material and its distribution; the establishment of common orthographies to enable production of literature in all the important languages of the Region; production of suitable English lessons for new literates wishing to learn English; Visual Aids as a means of public enlightenment, etc., etc.

Adult Literacy has since then become one aspect of the Adult Education Campaign. It is not all literacy classes. Provinces (there are 12) have been forging ahead with plans to incorporate the various means and agencies in the work.[1]

The Adult Education Officer (or, as he was termed at the time, Mass Education Officer) appointed in 1950 to take charge of the campaign was my brother, Wilfrid F. Jeffries, who had had long service in the Education Department of the Northern Region and had been in charge of a teacher training college at Bauchi, where he was a close friend of Nigeria's future prime minister, the late Sir Abubakar Tafawa Balewa, whose tragic death in 1966 was so grievous a loss to his country, and who was at that time headmaster of a school at Bauchi.

The campaign had to be designed and planned *ab initio*, for there was little in the way of documented experience elsewhere to afford guidance; and, in any case, the highly individual political and social character of the Region called for treatment specially adapted to its particular circumstances. In approaching the problem Wilfrid Jeffries states that he was guided by conclusions to which he had been led by experience and reflection. The first was that an all-out effort to eradicate illiteracy as a self-contained operation separated from normal educational or 'community development' programmes was a practical

47

necessity in order (as he paradoxically put it) to 'debunk' literacy. 'In the country of the blind the one-eyed man is king', says the proverb. When the greater part of a people is illiterate, and the country concerned has developed a complex and sophisticated form of government and is involved in economic and political relations with the outside world, the literates and semi-literates enjoy a power and privilege which are due merely to their possessing the art of literacy and are not necessarily justified by their personal merits or abilities. For example, illiterate persons—however qualified by intelligence or character—cannot be employed in public offices, even for clerical duties; while the opportunities opened up to unscrupulous literates to exploit their illiterate brethren are all too obvious. If such a situation is allowed to continue, there must result a widening gap between the 'haves' and the 'have-nots' within the community, and internal tensions can hardly fail to develop. Liberty and democracy cannot flourish in such conditions.

This was of special importance in the political situation as it existed at the time. Northern Nigeria, which continued to be divided into emirates ruled over by the traditional 'native authorities', was given, under a constitution introduced in 1947, a Regional House of Assembly with limited powers; and representatives of the Region sat in the Central Legislative Council which made laws for Nigeria as a whole. For various reasons, including the greater prevalence of illiteracy, the franchise arrangements in Northern Nigeria were more narrowly based than those in the other regions; and generally its rulers and political leaders felt that their Region was suffering handicaps which prevented it from exercising the authority in the councils of the country to which its size, population and natural resources entitled it. In so far as mass illiteracy was a contributor to these handicaps, the authorities had every incentive to do something about it.

For these reasons, a campaign designed to make all the people literate was fully justified and necessary quite apart from the advantages which individuals would gain in money or improved standards of life as a result of literacy. A second principle of no less importance than the first emerges at this stage of the argument, however: a campaign aimed at making people literate without also helping them to benefit from literacy would be uneconomic and unprofitable even if it could succeed at all. The literacy campaign, though self-contained with its own organisation and technical methods, must therefore be planted firmly in the context of a comprehensive system of adult education and supported by an adequate supply of reading matter, graduated in stages to correspond to the reader's growth in proficiency, but always conceived in adult terms. Since there was now a regional government which could give general directions, it was possible—as it would not have been before 1947—to plan the campaign on a regional basis and to provide central co-ordination, standardised methods of organisation and instruction, preparation of teaching material in the languages required and training in its use, and the inspection of field work. This central supervision was, at the outset, included in the portfolio of the Minister for Local Government and Community Development; later it was transferred to the Minister of Education and Social Services, and at this point the Adult Education staff took over the conduct of the campaign in the field from the administrative officers who had previously been responsible. The organisation of the field work was based upon the governmental structure of the Region. Each of the twelve provinces into which the Region was divided included a number of 'native authorities', and the principle adopted was that in each locality the literacy campaign was made the responsibility of the local native authority, whether this term denoted an emir or other personal ruler, or a duly constituted local government body. The function of the Adult Education staff, which was employed by the regional government, was to advise, co-ordinate and inspect.

A 'scheme' was prepared for each locality, covering a convenient area coinciding with a traditional social unit (or part of such a unit if it were too large). The scheme was the property of the native authority, which was responsible for carrying it out and was the direct employer of the organiser and the part-time instructors, receiving a grant from regional funds in aid of the costs. The scheme organiser was paid at the appropriate rate for an official of his standing in the service of the native authority concerned. The part-time instructors* were given a token reward, but as a matter of policy they were not paid salaries and were expected to be self-supporting in some normal trade or profession, in which they were encouraged to remain, in order that they should not be in difficulty when their part in the campaign was finished. No attempt was made to recruit instructors willing to give their services free of charge. The response would not have produced the numbers required, and the suggestion would have been out of keeping with custom. Wherever possible, private classes which had been started by public-spirited persons were absorbed into the campaign; this recognition was appreciated and the standard reward was gladly accepted as the equivalent of the gift traditionally bestowed by a chief upon those who have performed a service in the public interest.

Scheme organisers were locally recruited: the qualifications looked for were intelligence and personality rather than a high standard of school education. Most of the instructors, though literate, were men of very slight education, but it was found that under supervision they were capable of handling a suitable teaching method. It was definite policy not to employ primary school teachers and to use local officials ('tax mallams') only if they were suitable and willing. The main source of supply was people who had been to school and were working on their own account as farmers, traders or craftsmen. Classes were limited to twenty-five students; there were two sessions each year, and at the end of each session the classes were disbanded and new ones assembled, no students from the previous class being eligible for re-admission.

* The use of the term 'teacher' was deliberately avoided.

The local rulers effectively backed up the campaign, though at the outset a few of them, mindful of unfortunate past experience of trouble caused by semi-educated rascals, needed to be convinced of its desirability. Some would have preferred attendance at literacy classes to have been made compulsory by law, but it was generally agreed that it would be enough for people to be told that 'the Emir wishes it'. Momentum was quickly gained: hundreds of thousands of classes were set up in all parts of the Region and very large numbers of people were taught to read. So far as it went, the exercise was an undoubted success and a great boon to the country and its people. In the result, however, it fell far short of introducing anything like universal literacy; indeed, in Nigeria as a whole, the number of adult illiterates is estimated to have risen from about 13 million in 1950 to about 18 million in 1962; and it is reasonable to assume that at least half of these illiterates are in the Northern Region.

One reason for the campaign having been only partially successful would seem to be that, although it was planned and executed on a large scale, the resources behind it were at no time such as would have matched up to the immense task of making the whole people literate within a limited period. Another reason would seem to be that when, after a few years, the initial momentum had expended itself, literacy classes began to be treated as one of the routine activities of a local authority; the idea of an all-out drive faded away. Moreover, by 1956 or so, the main interest of the leaders in the Northern Region, as in other parts of Nigeria, was directed to constitutional issues, the campaign for independence and the struggle for political power in the Federation, rather than to domestic social concerns.

However this may be, the literacy effort did not fail, as some others have failed, for lack of attention to the need for providing the necessary follow-up in the shape of literature and adult education facilities for the new literates. Study kits were prepared and circulated. Film strips were produced dealing with practical health and agricultural problems and telling the people about

51

the country in which they lived. Copies of a calendar containing pictures of local interest sold, says Mallam Ahmadu Coomassie, 'like hot loaves'. The most ambitious venture, however, was the North Regional Literature Agency which was started in 1954 by Wilfrid Jeffries, who took on its direction, handing the literacy campaign over to Mallam Ahmadu Coomassie. Some particulars of its work are given in the appendix.

GHANA (GOLD COAST)

After Nigeria, the largest British colonial territory in West Africa was the Gold Coast, now the Republic of Ghana. Europeans are inclined to lump all Africans together in their minds (and Africans no doubt do the same for Europeans); but, though geographically near neighbours, Nigeria and the Gold Coast were (and are) about as alike in their social organisation and way of life as are, say, England and Spain. The Gold Coast was much the smaller country, being about the size of Britain, with a population, at the time, of about 4 million. It was relatively prosperous, supplying a large share of the world's consumption of cocoa and having also important mineral resources. Except in the far north, communications and social services were well developed and the standard of educational advancement was high for tropical Africa, but the bulk of the population, especially in the rural areas, was still illiterate.

The genesis of the literacy campaign in the Gold Coast was rather different from that of the Northern Nigerian campaign. After the war, the Gold Coast government and the Colonial Office set on foot a considerable effort to promote community development and the establishment of local government institutions as a means of social progress and political education. There was much concern amongst thinking people, both African and European, about the danger of the population's dividing into 'two nations'—an educated minority wielding economic and political power, and an illiterate proletariat living under conditions which might approach to serfdom. It was decided to appeal to the educated members of the population to undertake, as a matter of public service, to assist their less fortunate fellow citizens to share the benefits of education. To this end, a pilot scheme was introduced in the British mandated territory of Togoland which was administered by the Gold Coast government.

The basis of the Togoland scheme was an invitation to all teachers, clerks and other educated people to accept social responsibility and offer themselves for training and service as community leaders, without fee or salary or even payment of expenses. A short training course was devised, to be held successively at different centres as the team of instructors moved about the country. The course would cover agriculture, hygiene and physical training as well as literacy. All possible publicity was given to the venture, with the full co-operation of the large employers such as the United Africa Company. By 1949, the work was ready to begin and the first course started. An immediate surprise, however, awaited the organisers. No sooner was the course in being than the place in which it was held was invaded by hundreds of women from the villages around demanding that they should be taught to read. The women would not and could not be refused; improvised classes were set up, with every available literate person roped in as amateur teacher. Fortunately a primer in the Ewe language was available, though in nothing like sufficient numbers. It had been prepared on the advice of Dr Laubach following a visit which he had paid to lecture at Achimota College. This curious pattern was repeated at the centres where subsequent courses were held, as many as a thousand women sometimes descending upon the course. In the outcome, the general movement for community development which had been planned became very largely a literacy campaign. Considerable success was achieved but, as has so often happened, lack of follow-up material robbed the campaign of much of its potential effect.

The pilot scheme in Togoland was held to justify extension of the campaign to the whole country. Still under the general heading of community development, the government set up a departmental organisation to arrange for literacy teaching in the first instance, leading on from that to the wider question of community service. As in the pilot scheme, the basis was the recruitment and training of voluntary, unpaid teachers. The campaign was to be an intensive one lasting for three months, and the commitment of the volunteers would be limited to this period. At the end of the campaign, those who had passed the test of literacy would receive certificates, and their instructors would be given badges of honour indicating the numbers of persons whom they had taught to read. One idea which proved successful was the provision of a 'literacy kit', consisting of a primer, two follow-up reading books, a pencil, a notebook and a learner's badge, which was sold to the prospective student for 2s 6d.

The project aroused much public interest and enthusiasm. The newspapers owned by the *Daily Mirror* group gave it generous publicity, issuing the whole of the community development plan as a serial. The churches instituted a National Literacy Sunday and exhorted their congregations to co-operate. In fact, about 75 per cent of the volunteer teachers enrolled were obtained through the bodies constituting the National Christian Council.

The three-months' course was designed to bring the student up to the literacy standard proposed by UNESCO as the international standard for census purposes, namely ability to read with understanding a short passage about his everyday life in any language, and to write a simple letter. Certificates of literacy were awarded to those who succeeded in passing the test, and in order to maintain public interest the presentation of these certificates and of the instructors' badges of honour was made a ceremonial occasion. The people would gather at the appointed time and place, the presentation would be made by the chief or the district officer or some other notable, and general festivity would ensue. Amongst the wealthy cocoa farmers a custom had grown up of purchasing brass band instruments from England by mail order and organising local bands; there were some 200 of these aspiring bands at the time of the campaign but most of the members had little idea of how to make music with their strange instruments. There was a demand for help. The government agreed to second two instructors from the police band to train the local groups on one condition: that when they had learnt to play they would attend on the 'literacy days' and give the proceedings the appropriate musical background.

The first year's campaign was so successful that substantially the same pattern has been repeated annually. There have been steady increases in the numbers of students; on an average some 60 to 65 per cent have been women. No difficulty has been experienced in obtaining a constant supply of volunteer teachers. Some, as is to be expected, have occasionally fallen by the wayside, but as many as 70 per cent have faithfully completed the course entrusted to them. An effort was made to provide follow-up reading material in the form of a weekly newspaper, but it ran into difficulties of distribution.

The fact that the campaigns have had to be repeated annually over a long period shows that they cannot be classed as a successful attempt to eradicate illiteracy once and for all. According to the estimate in *World Illiteracy at Mid-Century*, the Gold Coast in 1950 had an adult population (fifteen years of age and over) of 2·5 million, of whom between 1·9 and 2 million (75–80 per cent) were illiterate.[2] The 1965 statistics show the adult illiterates in Ghana in 1962 as 1,434,000 males and 1,879,000 females representing percentages of 71 and 90 respectively.[3] The great majority of the illiterates are in the rural areas and in the higher age groups. The number of adults who learned to read in a year reached over 32,500 in 1955 but this figure was not attained in any subsequent year up to 1964. The average was about 22,500. It would not appear, therefore, that advance has been any faster since independence was attained in 1957 than under the British colonial régime.

Meanwhile, however, great progress has been made in Ghana in developing the formal education of children. By 1960, 74 per cent of the boys and 37 per cent of the girls of ten years of age were enrolled in schools, and the average annual increase in school enrolment was running at over 9 per cent. At this rate illiteracy will disappear from Ghana in the foreseeable future as the percentage of the population that has had a school education increases. However, a good deal more than the sort of adult literacy campaigns undertaken in the past needs to be done in order to accelerate the process to a significant extent, and a new national effort has now been put in hand by the Ghana government.

UGANDA

If there are differences between territories near to each other in West Africa, these are small compared with the differences between the opposite coasts of the continent. A literacy worker who crossed to East Africa after a period of service on the West Coast described the transition as like a journey to a different world. In the Gold Coast—apart perhaps from the remoter northern areas—a social organisation of a high order existed. The people were grouped under chiefs in identifiable 'village' communities, with strong ties of kinship and neighbourhood and a way of life based on traditional rules and customs. If one were to look at Uganda in the 1950s, one would find an entirely different state of affairs. Instead of congregating in villages (which in the Gold Coast were often more what we should call towns), the people were scattered over the countryside in small groups living in 'shambas', with little communication between one hamlet and the next except a rough jungle footpath, and with little or no organised social hierarchy. As in the Gold Coast, a complex diversity of languages added to the difficulty.

Before, therefore, literacy work could begin in Uganda, it was necessary to create the focal points which in such a country as the Gold Coast were ready-made. In the 1940s, Miss C. I. M.

Hastie arrived in the country as a welfare officer.* She set to work to form clubs for women, whose position in Uganda was traditionally subordinate to that of the men—another contrast with the Gold Coast, where women enjoyed considerable influence and prestige. The opportunity offered by the new clubs was eagerly seized in spite of some grumbling from the male sex, and the movement swept the country. At first the activities of the clubs were concerned with domestic subjects—child care, needlework, cooking and the rest—but, once the groups were established, literacy teaching was successfully introduced. In time the men were stirred to emulate their consorts, and formed their own clubs and literacy classes.

A. R. G. Prosser, CMG, MBE, now Adviser on Social Welfare to the Ministry of Overseas Development, who was responsible for literacy work successively in the Gold Coast and Uganda, and to whom I am greatly indebted for the information here recorded about those countries, relates a touching incident relating to the Uganda classes. When travelling in a remote part of the country, his car was stopped by an African who pressed him to take a short walk to visit the local literacy class. The short walk, Prosser found, involved a tramp of several miles along a jungle path, and the crossing of a river by somewhat primitive and acrobatic methods. At length his guide led him to a place where some eighteen people, men and women, were assembled. The leader introduced them in very passable English and proudly produced their textbook. This class, which had been formed spontaneously and without any official sponsorship or encouragement, was painstakingly teaching itself to read and write English with the sole aid of an extremely battered children's primer, of Victorian date and with text and illustrations such as would make any modern educationist throw up his hands in horror. How this relic found its way from some English family to that isolated settlement in the very heart of Africa must remain a mystery. Yet so

* Later she became Assistant Commissioner and Adviser on Women's community development, and was awarded the MBE.

great was the desire for literacy and so fiery the enthusiasm of the leader that, even with this poor tool, the job was being done.

Under the auspices of Y. K. Lule, the African Minister for Social Development, a system of rural training centres covering the sixteen districts of Uganda was established during the late nineteen-fifties. These formed focal points for the recruitment and training of literacy organisers. The Christian denominations helped by training their catechists to teach literacy and setting up literacy classes at every local church and mission station. The campaign had the advantage of being able to draw upon the already existing East African Literature Bureau (the work of which will be referred to in Chapter 10) for primers, readers and general literary material, so that this could be ready in time to meet the demand when it came. Use was made of a series of instructional publications in the main vernaculars, produced in newspaper form through the good offices of the *East African Standard*. These covered such matters as the cultivation of cotton and coffee. Illustrated by cartoon drawings, they proved very popular. They were given away free to people who had earned them, for example, by attendance at classes; their possession gave some prestige to the holder.

Generally, the story of literacy in Uganda has been one of quiet and unspectacular progress, with none of the flamboyance which marked the effort in the Gold Coast. Uganda's illiteracy problem is not yet solved; in 1962, half of the men and three-quarters of the women in the country were still in the illiterate category. Even so, by tropical African standards, Uganda has made a good start and is on the way to overcoming the problem.

These illustrations from former British territories in Africa (and I must emphasise that they are only intended as illustrations: no disparagement is implied of other efforts, British or non-British, which I have omitted to catalogue) show a clear tendency towards the conception of a literacy programme in terms of the vernacular language of the people. It is, however, of interest to note that the people themselves, after gaining some experience, have not always found it satisfactory to let the matter rest there. In Uganda, where there are some seventy different languages or dialects, English is the official language and the *lingua franca*. Without literacy in English, people cannot advance very far in education or culture. Realising this, the Uganda Council of Women, once again taking the lead, successfully applied to UNESCO in 1960 for expert help in planning a programme for the teaching of English to adult women.

FRENCH-SPEAKING AFRICA

In the French-speaking territories of Africa there appears to have been a more conscious and deliberate movement to make knowledge of, and literacy in, the French language the ultimate objective of the programme. Although such a policy involves many difficulties, it reduces others: for example, it becomes unnecessary to defer the teaching of literacy until in the fullness of time every vernacular has been rendered into writing. It is of interest to compare the experience of the French-speaking country of Niger with that already recorded of Nigeria a decade earlier. The story of the Niger programme is related by M. Jean Meyer in the periodical *Coopération Pédagogique* of the French Ministry of Education.[4]

Niger, in 1961, had a population of 3 million, of whom over 95 per cent were illiterate. The government appealed to UNESCO to provide an expert to advise on the planning and execution of an adult literacy programme. On his advice a *Bureau de l'alphabétisation et éducation des adultes* was set up in the Ministry of Education, and plans were drawn up for a pilot scheme, covering in the first instance ten villages. The success of this scheme justified the government in going ahead with a broad programme, beginning with a hundred villages in 1963-64 and a hundred more in each succeeding year until the whole country could be covered. In each district a regional committee was constituted, under the presidency of the *commandant de cercle* and including representatives of the local technical services (agriculture, health, education, etc.). The committees were responsible for the payment of the instructors, who received a modest remuneration for the four months (January to May in each year) occupied by the courses. These instructors were recruited from the teaching profession, the medical and agricultural auxiliary services, and educated members of the public. Courses of training for them were instituted in 1964. Buildings to serve as classrooms were put up by the villagers themselves, and each centre was equipped by the government with a blackboard, a radio, a film strip projector and screen, a terrestrial globe, maps of Africa and of Niger, and a supply of notebooks and ball-point pens for the students. A specially designed periodical, entitled *Savoir pour mieux vivre*, was prepared for the benefit of both teachers and learners.

The scheme was worked out on a two-year plan. The first-year course, running from January to May, was designed to bring the student to the point of being able to read specially prepared literature intelligently, to acquire a basic French vocabulary, and to absorb incidentally a certain amount of useful general information. The course consisted of fifteen lessons—one for each week—devised to cover two sessions of one hour plus a period devoted to conversation, this last being arranged to fit in with a special radio broadcast. In these lessons the basic medium of instruction was a film strip of twelve frames, and the instructor was provided with detailed directions as to how to use it at each successive repetition and how to progress from the vernacular to the French language in his question-and-answer dialogue with the class. The villages where the first-year course had taken place went on in the following January to the second-year course, while other villages were beginning the first stage. This second course included the use of more advanced literature, with emphasis on collective reading. Further progress would be made with the French language, with writing, and with the acquisition of knowledge that would help the people to improve their standards of living. After completing this course, the villagers should be able to maintain without external assistance a permanent adult education centre, where those who had been taught could go on to teach others, which would serve as a focal point for community development.

Another French-speaking African territory of special interest in the context of the struggle against illiteracy is the Ivory Coast. This republic was the country chosen as the scene of a notable pilot project concerning the use of television for literacy teaching. The thinking behind this project, which is particularly associated with the name of the late Gaston Berger,* was based on the calculation that, in order to meet the basic educational needs of the people who will be living in the world in AD 2000, it will be necessary to increase the number of schools from 2 million to 4 million, and the number of qualified teachers from 10 million to 25 million. Even so, this tremendous expansion would only suffice to provide an educational standard already considered inadequate for mid-century conditions, and would be likely to be found even more inadequate for the conditions of forty years ahead. Such a prospect makes it very necessary to take advantage of whatever help can be given by the new instruments which science has made available and which need no longer be considered as mere auxiliaries to the teacher's work but can (to a certain extent and subject to certain limitations) take the place of the professional teacher, with resulting economy in skilled man-power.

In the African countries associated with France, a good deal of experience was accumulated, from 1956 onwards, in the use of radio for literacy teaching. A method, known as radiovision, was developed, in which film strips were shown to the classes in synchronisation with special broadcast programmes. From this it was a natural step to the use of television. The immense possibilities of reaching a wide audience by this medium are

* Gaston Berger, philosopher and expert on higher education, was President of the French Commission for UNESCO until his death in 1960.

obvious; so are the difficulties which are encountered in practice. Perhaps the least of these, though formidable enough, is the necessity of providing suitable transmitters and receiving sets in countries where much of the population is scattered in widely separated villages and settlements without main supplies of electricity. That is a physical difficulty which can be overcome, but other difficulties, less tangible, are no less real. The wider the area it is sought to cover, the less easy it becomes to devise programmes which, in language and in presentation, will appeal equally to all the potential viewers. Even where French is well established as the official language and *lingua franca*, it has been found in many parts of Africa that the people for whom literacy instruction is needed still rely upon a diversity of vernaculars and do not know enough French to be capable of receiving instruction in that tongue. Again, teaching by television has the special disadvantage that, if the student happens to miss a lesson or two—as he all too probably will—he has lost his place and cannot very easily catch up.

It was with such problems as these in mind that the French Ministries of Education and Co-operation sponsored a series of experiments conducted by C. Chicot in the Ivory Coast between 1963 and 1965. Details are contained in a collection of documents which the Institut National Pédagogique very kindly put at my disposal, but I must content myself here with a few general observations. Among the devices used to test out methods was an arrangement by which a lesson being given to one class was transmitted 'live' by closed-circuit television to another class of pupils of the same educational level, and the reactions of the latter carefully studied. Other experiments concerned the possibility of training by television people who could act as instructors and organise local 'teleclubs' in their neighbourhood; others again were aimed at discovering how far and how best television could be employed to teach spoken French.

Definite results have not been claimed, and could not be expected, from a pilot project of this kind. There can be no doubt, however, that as time goes on television, especially with the additional facilities which will be opened up by the development of satellite communication, will have an increasing part to play in the educational field. The Ivory Coast experiments have clearly made a significant initial contribution to the study of the potentialities of the new medium in the particular context of literacy teaching.

It is noticeable that, whereas in the Soviet campaign of the 1920s and in Laubach's pioneer efforts, the primary—indeed the sole—aim had been the eradication of illiteracy, considered as constituting an end in itself (a conception which also underlay the Northern Nigerian campaign of the 1950s), a somewhat different approach marked the programmes undertaken in both English and French speaking territories in Africa in the 1960s. In these programmes we find the teaching of literacy regarded as an element—an important and indispensable element, but still one element amongst others—in a general movement for social and cultural community development. This reflects a certain shift in expert opinion due largely to the fact that a number of literacy campaigns, embarked upon with much enthusiasm and high hopes, had proved disappointingly unproductive of lasting results. Northern Nigeria, as has been observed above, is indeed a case in point. Several of the earlier Indian campaigns lapsed before making a significant impact, and the progress of literacy there has fallen very far short of the possibilities so confidently envisaged by Laubach in 1940. Haiti, where it was at one time possible to claim that a literacy campaign was 'in process of transforming' the country,[5] has yet remained one of the areas most hard hit by illiteracy.

No one cause, it would seem, accounts for all the failures. Many are rightly ascribed to lack of adequate provision for following up the initial impetus and for making available sufficient supplies of suitable reading material, but this was not everywhere the case. Sometimes unforeseen political developments have altered the course of events. Campaigns successfully initiated by missionary or philanthropic enterprise have not always secured the official moral and financial support necessary to enable the work to be pursued with adequate resources. In the opinion of some authorities the much-advertised 'each one teach one' principle has proved somewhat illusory. It is held, in the light of experience, that a more skilled and professional organisation of teaching is necessary and that literacy instruction must be integrated with continuing programmes of general adult education. On the other hand, there are those who maintain that there was nothing wrong with the earlier approach, and that it can and will lead to success if—and this is an essential condition—it is carried through to the end. The difference between a nation or community which for practical purposes is *wholly* literate and one in which only a part, even though it be a substantial part, of the population is literate is a difference not of degree but of kind. A nation or community which has, once and for all, put illiteracy behind it has entered a new dimension of social development, and all its plans and policies can start from a new forward base. When and where conditions make it practicable to undertake an intensive all-out drive with the single purpose of completely eradicating illiteracy, this may well be worth while, even if other desirable activities have to be left on one side for the time being. They will have all the better chance of being effectively pursued when literacy has been established.

In illustration of this point, particular interest attaches to the literacy campaign carried out in 1961 in Cuba. An account of it is contained in the report of a UNESCO mission which visited the island in 1964.[6]

CUBA

The population of Cuba at present is rather more than 7 million. When the country became independent in 1899, the census showed that nearly 57 per cent of the population was illiterate. By 1953, the figure had dropped to 23 per cent, but this average figure conceals a marked difference between the rates for the urban and rural areas, which were respectively 11 and 41.7 per cent.

When the revolutionary government took control in 1959, one of the first tasks it set itself was the eradication of illiteracy, more particularly in the rural districts. This had a double purpose. It would promote the economic and cultural progress of a country suffering from underdevelopment, and dependent upon agriculture and on finding means to exploit its as yet untapped mineral resources. At the same time, teaching people to read and write afforded an opportunity for instructing them in the ideas and policies of the revolutionary movement. This revolutionary motivation provided inspiration for both teachers and taught, and was a valuable factor in bringing the campaign to a successful conclusion. It is no disparagement to a great effort to point out that other factors combined to create conditions far more favourable than those met with in many other countries. The illiteracy problem, though serious, was of a manageable size. The government was strong, determined and powerful enough to see that its wishes were carried out. Above all, there was no language problem, since Spanish is the established language of the country. Nevertheless, to deal with the problem in one short, sharp year was a notable achievement.

The initiation of the campaign was announced by the head of the government, Fidel Castro, at the United Nations General Assembly in September 1960, and intensive preparations were set on foot at once for action in 1961, which was later designated as the 'Year of Education'. The direction of the campaign was entrusted to a National Literacy Commission. The last four months of 1960 saw the preparatory stage of the campaign. The Commission produced $1\frac{1}{2}$ million copies of a specially designed illustrated primer comprising fifteen lessons and entitled *Venceremos* (We shall Conquer). A teaching manual for the instructors (*alfabetizadores*) was also prepared, covering not only literacy teaching but 'a clear exposition of twenty-four revolutionary orientation themes'.

At the same time steps were being taken to recruit, train and organise those who would teach. The principle adopted was: 'The People should teach the People'—in other words, the main work was to be done by voluntary, unpaid instructors, working under the technical guidance of professional teachers. The instructors came from various sources. Members of the public provided, during the course of the year, 120,632 *alfabetizadores*. The Conrado Benitez Students Brigade provided 100,000, and the *Patria o Muerte* Workers Brigade some 15,000. The professional teachers who supervised and trained these volunteers numbered 34,772. Thus, in all, well over a quarter of a million people were actively involved in the campaign. The government provided a credit of 13 million pesos, which was supplemented by voluntary contributions from the supporting organisations and the public.

The first phase (January to March 1961) was chiefly devoted to the establishment of the field organisation and to an intensive publicity drive, utilising all available media: press, radio, television, public meetings and so on. This was designed both to stimulate recruitment of instructors and to enlist the enthusiastic co-operation of the illiterate population. The slogan was: 'If you can teach, teach; if you can't teach, learn.' Campaign hymns and songs were composed and circulated.

As might be expected, all kinds of difficulties were encountered, not least the difficulty of identifying the illiterates, many of whom were not keen to disclose their ignorance. The difficulties, however, were tackled with vigour and not allowed to impede the progress of the campaign. In the first phase, the volunteer instructors drawn from the general public were the mainstay of the work. From April 1961 onwards, they were reinforced by the young student *brigadistas*, and later by workers drawn from factories. The pattern aimed at during the second phase (April to August) was to assign two illiterate pupils to each *alfabetizador*. During this phase, the gaps in organisation were filled up and more and more instructors trained and sent

66

out into the field. This has been described as the most constructive stage of the campaign. It culminated in a National Literacy Congress held at the beginning of September, after which the campaign moved into its final and most intensive phase.

On November 5, 1961, came the first announcement that a municipality was free from illiteracy. Others followed thick and fast in a spirit of competition. As one was declared free, the instruction teams moved on to others which were behind. On December 22, at a great public meeting, Cuba was solemnly declared to have eradicated illiteracy: 707,000 persons had been taught to read and write. Granted that, as has been pointed out, the conditions were favourable, it was a remarkable feat to have accomplished so much in a few short months. The UNESCO Commission wrote: 'The secret of the success of the Campaign must be found in a very simple fact, one that is very old and foreign to all technical means: human relationships. It must be found in those intellectual, sentimental and psychological chain reactions, which arise when relations are established between one human being and another.'[7]

In a crash programme carried out in so brief a space of time, the learner could only be brought to an elementary stage of literacy. During 1961, preparation for the follow-up of the campaign had been put in hand; and from 1962 onwards, a programme of post-literacy and adult education courses was planned and conducted by what was called the Worker-Farmer Education National Office. The content of these courses was both practical and ideological. A variant of the scheme, designed to suit people who were not keen to attend courses, was the establishment of 'home reading circles', meeting under the guidance of amateur teachers. Large quantities of special reading matter were produced and circulated, and full use was made of radio and television for adult education purposes.

Difficulties were encountered, and overcome, in Cuba which have a bearing on the general question of literacy campaigns.

The special organisation which had been created to carry out the literacy teaching was disbanded at the end of 1961, when its immediate task had been completed, and there was a hiatus before the worker-farmer education scheme got into its stride. This break in continuity hampered the start of the post-literacy work and there was some fear about the end of 1962 that the initial impulse had been lost. However, from the spring of 1963 onwards, the statistics began to show a gradual but steady improvement.

In this chapter I have given a few examples of the local or national programmes which were carried out, on varying scales and with varying success in many countries between 1954 and 1961. Different methods had been tried out and much experience had been gained. Inevitably, there was a good deal of wastage and disappointment; but in many places substantial numbers of people had learned to read and write, and definite signs of social progress could be distinguished. These local efforts were the curtain-raisers to a drama which would henceforth be played out on the world stage.

6

UNESCO TAKES A HAND

THE WORK of the United Nations Educational, Scientific and Cultural Organisation, commonly known as UNESCO, covers a wide field; but, from the beginning of its activities at the end of the Second World War, the problem of illiteracy has been one of its main preoccupations.

In the early days of UNESCO, scientific study of the problem was, as has been seen, still in its infancy. There was still no accepted terminology or exact definition of the various aspects of the subject. Expressions such as 'adult education', 'mass education', 'fundamental education', 'community development' were linked in different parts of the world with a wide variety of activities. The same term might be found to mean different things in different places, or different terms in practice might mean the same thing. Recognition of illiteracy as constituting a problem in its own right (though not one that can be considered in isolation from other educational and social problems) did not come about for some years.

Moreover, UNESCO was still feeling its way towards the right demarcation of functions within itself. 'Adult education' was a small division of the organisation. 'Fundamental education' was dealt with separately, and was conceived in terms of providing 'useful knowledge and basic training to those who had not had the advantages of schooling'. Later, this 'fundamental education' was considered as part of 'community development', which concerned the United Nations Bureau of Social Affairs as well as UNESCO.

During the 1950s, however, there were two movements heralding a different approach. The term 'fundamental education' was dropped, and gradually the term 'adult education' was recognised as covering all organised provision for the education of adults at all levels, from the simplest to the most sophisticated. It embraced, therefore, literacy teaching for the illiterate as well as 'further', 'higher' or 'liberal' education for adults who have already received normal schooling. At the same time, there was growing recognition of literacy as constituting a field in itself—as, in fact, presenting one of the major basic problems confronting the world.

In all the countries included in the colonial empires or special spheres of influence of the great powers, the wind of change was blowing. Soon after the end of the Second World War, India, Pakistan, Burma, the Philippines and Ceylon became fully independent. The British concession of independence to the Gold Coast (Ghana) and the Federation of Malaya in 1957 opened a decade in which colonial constitutions tumbled like ninepins. The British, French and Belgian possessions in Africa, French Indochina, Dutch Indonesia, the British Borneo territories, along with Trinidad, Jamaica, British Guiana, Cyprus, Mauritius and many more islands and territories, were in a short space of time recognised or on the point of being recognised as sovereign independent states and received into membership of the United Nations.

The role of UNESCO is only to a limited extent that of a direct provider of financial assistance for member states. Its principal function is to act as a central agency, at the service of all, for inspiring, planning and co-ordinating action, for pooling information and experience, for conducting and if necessary subsidising research and experiment, and for providing member governments, as required, with facts, figures, expert advice, technical help and its general good offices, in order that national programmes may be wisely prepared and efficiently conducted. The organisation carries out its task in a number of ways. At its

70

headquarters in Paris UNESCO maintains a staff of experienced persons, drawn from a variety of national and professional backgrounds. It collects and analyses factual and statistical data, and publishes the results for general information and use. It convenes *ad hoc* and standing committees of eminent authorities to advise on various aspects of its work: one such is the International Committee of Experts on Literacy. It organises research projects and pilot schemes in association with national governments and academic institutions. Directly or through its branch offices, it arranges conferences, seminars and other gatherings for discussion at different levels and in different parts of the world as circumstances may require, providing the background material and often the secretarial organisation. And from its presses there comes a wealth of authoritative studies, handbooks, memoranda and other documents for the benefit of planners, organisers and field workers concerned in national programmes.

If it was a coincidence, it was a fortunate one that the year 1957, which ushered in the revolutionary decade, also saw the culmination of years of intensive work which were crowned by the publication of the impressive statistical survey to which I have already referred: *World Illiteracy at Mid-Century*. A preliminary study of the progress of literacy in twenty-six selected countries had already appeared, but the new publication was the first systematic attempt to set forth all the known facts about illiteracy in all the countries of the world. The preface to the 1957 survey contains the following passage:

As long as more than two-fifths of the world's adult population cannot read or write in any language, and are thus deprived of their full participation in the cultural life of mankind, the question of world illiteracy must continue to be of concern to all. Furthermore, progress in the reduction of illiteracy is closely related to other aspects of educational, social and economic progress of a community, a country, or of the world as a whole. Hence it is essential to consider the question of illiteracy, not as an isolated phenomenon, but in all its inter-relationship with other factors of modernisation.[1]

This observation states the two principles which have since become generally accepted: first, that the eradication of illiteracy is in itself a necessary and distinct operation: but, secondly, that it is pointless to undertake it in a vacuum. In the words of an African conference held in 1964: 'Literacy should not be regarded as an end in itself, but only as a step in a programme of continuing education that enables men and women to take on more responsibilities and to play a more active role in society.'[2]

Some indication has already been given of the range of *World Illiteracy at Mid-Century*, which is an indispensable basic document for any student of the subject. Before proceeding to statistics, it discusses the various possible definitions of illiteracy and the methods of identifying and counting the illiterates in a population. Next, an attempt is made to estimate the number and percentage of illiterates, aged fifteen and over, for every country of the world, about 1950. The major areas of illiteracy, and the areas where illiteracy, though less prevalent, exists to a significant extent, are then examined in detail. Finally, there are chapters on the relations between illiteracy and school enrolment, national incomes and urban industrialisation; and some pointers are given to the directions in which further study and research are required.

By the late 1950s, the problem of illiteracy was at last beginning to be recognised as one of first-class international importance. At the General Assembly of the United Nations in December 1961, a resolution was carried inviting UNESCO 'to make a general review, at a regular session of its General Conference, of the question of the eradication of mass illiteracy throughout the world, with the object of working out concrete and effective measures, at the international and national levels, for such eradication'.[3] This challenge met with an active response from UNESCO. A report entitled *World Campaign for Universal Literacy* was prepared with as much speed as the range and complexity of the subject allowed, and was presented in person by the Director-General, René Maheu, to the Second Committee of the General Assembly in October 1963.

The report pointed out that, apart from the problem of existing adult illiteracy, the position of child illiteracy was alarming. Out of a total of 205 million children in eighty-five countries of Africa, Asia and Latin America, in 1960, only 110 million—or about 55 per cent—were attending primary schools, and a considerable proportion of these did not complete their schooling and fairly soon relapsed into illiteracy. As a result the illiterate adult population was now growing at the rate of 20 to 25 million a year.

> It is not a pretty picture, but it is one which we must have the courage to face. . . . There is isolated action at the national level varying in intensity and scope. But there is no universal effort commensurate with the global nature of this scourge and with what the whole earth stands to gain by its elimination. That is what is lacking and that is what UNESCO proposes considering.[4]

The main theme of the report was that, if adult and child illiteracy were to be wiped out, the battle must be waged on both these fronts at once. Free and compulsory education for children must be established everywhere so that the world should not be 'continuously flooded with new waves of illiterates'; but there must at the same time be a large-scale adult literacy campaign. Each operation was essential for the success of the other.

The plan put forward was an ambitious and far-reaching one. Assuming the current number of illiterate adults in the member states to be 500 million, UNESCO considered that it would be possible within ten years to make literate two-thirds of them—330 million—representing the active population aged between fifteen and fifty. This could be done by a combination of national effort and international aid, contributed to the local governments partly through UNESCO but for the most part bilaterally from individual states. About 75 per cent of the total effort should, it was thought, be put up by the governments of the countries concerned; the balance of 25 per cent would be the measure of the external aid required. It was roughly estimated that the cost of making a person literate would vary from 5\frac{1}{4}$ to 7\frac{1}{2}$—say £2–3 in round figures—depending on the region concerned. To deal with 330 million people would therefore cost $1,911 million—around £700 million—over the ten-year period.

To find three-quarters of this sum, UNESCO considered, was not outside the capabilities of the countries concerned, even taking into account the weakness of their economies. It would represent only 0.14 per cent of the gross national product of those countries in 1961, and could be brought within the scope of their development plans. External aid would call for $430 million, of which $330 million—$33 million a year—would be provided bilaterally, that is to say by direct arrangement between a donor and a receiver government. (It was observed that the total amount of bilateral aid provided for development in 1962 was $5,400 million.) This would leave $100 million to be found over the ten years by international action proper. 'If the international community so desires', said the Director-General, 'it will be possible, for the first time in history, for hundreds of millions of completely uneducated men and women to be given access to that education which is their absolute right.'[5] René Maheu went on to point out that the Universal Declaration of Human Rights had stated that everyone has the right to education, yet, fifteen years later, hundreds of millions of people could not read the sentence in which their sacred right was proclaimed. He also pointed out, very cogently, the danger to peace created by the widening inequality 'separating that part of mankind which enjoys the benefits of education and participates in the advances of science from the part which, not having access to the former, admires the latter without understanding them; that inequality which divides mankind into those who make history and are opening up the road to the stars and those who endure history and whose horizons are bounded by the ancestral routine'.[6]

The report thus presented was fully debated. Some national representatives were in favour of accepting the need for drastic action to eradicate illiteracy once and for all. The practical difficulty was that, although the Assembly could approve a plan, it could not enforce acceptance of the plan or of the consequential obligations by the countries which would have to find the bulk of the cost. Neither the 'donor' countries, nor indeed those faced with the problem of illiteracy, felt themselves to be in a position there and then to commit themselves to a definite programme of action and expenditure. Important as literacy was, there were many other calls in this 'development decade' (as the 1960s were called) on the available resources, and many other contestants in the battle for priority.

While, therefore, the report evoked what UNESCO justly considered to be 'a very gratifying response', the actual resolution passed by the General Assembly—1937 (XVIII) of December 11, 1963—was necessarily couched in rather general and permissive terms. It expressed appreciation of the report and deep concern at the grave situation revealed in it. It reaffirmed its belief that the right to education is one of the fundamental rights of man, and that mass illiteracy was an obstacle to social and economic progress during the development decade and thereafter. Recognising that, while the eradication of illiteracy is in the main a problem requiring national effort, intensified international co-operation was also called for, the resolution invited member states in which illiteracy was still widespread to accord appropriate priority in their development plans to the eradication of illiteracy and also, where necessary, to establish national programmes for continuing education for adults. The resolution also invited other states to help these national efforts with technical and/or financial assistance, and it invited the collaboration of non-governmental organisations active or interested in the field of education. It commended the work of UNESCO and encouraged the organisation to go forward with it, including the planning, supervision and financing of pilot projects. Finally, it invited the Secretary-General of the United Nations, in collaboration with the Director-General of UNESCO and heads of other organisations concerned with technical assistance and finance, to explore ways and means of supporting national efforts for the eradication of illiteracy by a world campaign and by any other measures, if appropriate, of international co-operation and assistance, both non-financial and financial, and to report to the Assembly, with appropriate proposals, at its next session.[7]

With this mandate behind them, the activities of UNESCO were quickly extended in range and intensity. In a series of personal discussions between the Director-General and heads of state, political leaders and other eminent authorities—including His Holiness Pope Paul VI, who promised his personal support for an intensification of UNESCO's work in this connection—literacy was an important topic.[8] A number of regional and national conferences were organised. The United Nations Economic Commission for Africa, meeting in February 1964, recorded its view that mass illiteracy is a grave handicap to social and economic development, and urged its member and associated governments to include programmes for adult literacy and adult education in their development plans. Similar recommendations were made about the same time by the United Nations Economic Commission for Asia and the Far East, and by the Conference of Arab National Commissions for UNESCO which, amongst other things, proposed the establishment of a special fund to which all the Arab countries would contribute.

In March 1964, a very important regional conference on the planning and organisation of literacy programmes in Africa was held at Abidjan, Ivory Coast. It was attended not only by representatives of thirty-five African countries, but by observers from several other parts of the world and from a number of non-governmental organisations. The report of this conference is an excellent statement of the principles and considerations that are involved in dealing with the problem of illiteracy in modern conditions. In various forms, these principles and considerations have already been noted in this book or will come to light in future pages; I shall not, therefore, attempt to recapitulate them here. What was brought out very clearly was the sheer inadequacy of the resources available to most of the African governments for dealing with this 'major scourge'. The conference accordingly adopted a resolution proposing that the United Nations should 'redouble its efforts to convince the advanced countries that they should devote a large share of their national income to cultural and technical co-operation and to the economic and social progress of the developing countries'.[9]

In August and September 1964, the Third Commonwealth Education Conference took place at Ottawa, Canada. This conference, like its predecessors, covered questions of Commonwealth co-operation in all fields of education, but on this occasion, for the first time, adult illiteracy was discussed, and the view was recorded that the eradication of illiteracy should form part of national policy. A committee of the conference considered the question of literacy in some detail, and its conclusions were appended to the conference report. While emphasising that measures for extending formal school education for young people at all levels should not be sacrificed in the interests of literacy for adults, the committee doubted whether formal school education and adult literacy need be thought of as real alternatives. The basis for literacy work already existed in programmes of community development, and, while the available machinery might need to be expanded, it was there.[10]

It has to be remembered that this was an education conference consisting almost entirely of members concerned politically or professionally with education, which generally signifies formal education. Nevertheless, the conference performed a useful service by laying stress on the need for adequate preparation of literacy programmes, for the production of special textbooks adapted to the needs of adult instruction, and for 'very special attention' to the necessity for 'the production, if necessary specially and locally, of reading matter for the new literate which arises from or is relevant to his own interests and environment, and which may need to be written in a local language'.[11] Reference was made to the British government's offer to collaborate with developing countries in pilot projects which 'would be conducted in depth in a few chosen and limited areas with the fullest complement of staff, aid, equipment and services'.[12] In commending such projects, the conference was, as will be seen, anticipating the general approach to the problem of illiteracy which UNESCO was proceeding to develop.

In the United States, a notable contribution to knowledge and thought concerning the problem of illiteracy was made by a working conference arranged, in May 1964, by the Center for Applied Linguistics on behalf of the Agency for International Development (AID) of the State Department. In this conference American official and academic experts were joined by colleagues from UNESCO and from India. Its purpose was twofold: to produce an outline of research needs, with emphasis on projects which AID might support under its research programme; and to provide 'guidelines' for use by AID in handling literacy problems in various national situations. The recommendations of the conference were embodied in a report—*Recommendations of the World Conference on Literacy*—edited and prepared by Alfred S. Hayes of the Center.

On the research side, thirty-one projects were identified as meriting consideration. I need not refer to them in detail here, but some general points which emerged call for notice. Attention was drawn to two serious gaps in knowledge. One was the 'almost total lack of any historical dimension in discussions of literacy in the developing countries'. The examination of the conditions under which literacy had been diffused and, equally important, maintained within the more advanced nations would be a major task of documentary analysis and would be generally enlightening even if some of the circumstances common enough in the early Western world were not reproduced in the developing countries of today. In particular, 'there could well be profound implications for literacy programs in the specific study of more recently developed countries such as Japan and Mexico'.[13] Another gap was caused by the lack of any systematic attempt to draw together the widely scattered, but nevertheless existing, documents containing the case histories of the successful and unsuccessful literacy projects so far undertaken, so as to provide a composite evaluation of what had already been done and help to prevent repetition of past errors. Research in the field of literacy involves a number of different disciplines accustomed to use differing techniques. Interdisciplinary understanding is essential; so is the planning of research in such a way as to be clearly related to practical problems. These considerations led the conference to the conclusion that the most productive source and proving ground for research was 'the learner in action'. 'Close observation and analysis of the behavior of the learner as he goes through the "curriculum" both tests previous research findings and stimulates new research directly related to his problems.'[14]

Among much useful technical guidance, the conference report includes some important statements of principle. No literacy programme can be considered completely successful unless it continues until its trainees reach a level of achievement which is 'self-sustaining'; that is to say, at which they continue to read and write as part of their daily living. 'One must learn to read until one can read to learn. This takes time.' Long-range planning is essential; so also is adequate preparation. 'The world is littered with the debris' of large-scale campaigns hastily launched with a view to quick results. 'Where little or no preparation has been made and few facilities or materials exist, it is

79

generally most inadvisable to announce the start of a literacy program or to expect actual teaching to begin in less than two years from the time the decision is taken and budget voted.'[15]

By September 1964, the UNESCO secretariat was in a position to draw up a report for consideration by the General Conference of the organisation due to take place in October 1964. The meetings and discussions leading up to this had to some extent dashed the hopes of those who had envisaged the resolution of the General Assembly as heralding an immediate all-out world attack on illiteracy with the purpose of eradicating it within a definite limit of time. True, the importance of dealing with illiteracy was now generally accepted in principle; but it was found to be another matter to translate that acceptance into practical decisions by getting individual governments to allocate to this purpose the necessary proportion of the scarce resources which had to be stretched to cover development of all kinds. To put the issue bluntly, an all-out campaign against illiteracy could only be undertaken at the expense of other urgent and vital projects. It is not the experts who have to decide priorities but the politicians who administer the national funds and the taxpayers who produce the funds. It might be good sense to hold up the provision of schools, hospitals and other services until the conquest of illiteracy was accomplished, but this is obviously not a very saleable proposition.

It was not only a matter of finding the money, however. Another and perhaps more important point was an increasing doubt whether merely to teach people to read and write, though essential, may not be a waste of effort unless it is part of a more general plan aimed at creating conditions in which the people can use their new skill. This implies the need for organised schemes not only for providing suitable and accessible reading matter, but for relating literacy to opportunities for training and promotion.

7

TEHERAN—A TURNING POINT?

BASED ON a reappraisal of the situation in the light of these considerations, the report of the secretariat circulated to members of the UNESCO General Conference in September 1964 outlined 'the broad lines of a new policy' and described 'the operational plan for World Literacy in which the Director-General proposed to give form and reality to this policy'.[1]

The new approach to the problem was 'a selective strategy— a strategy of intensive projects rather than of extensive campaigns'. The eradication of mass illiteracy remained the final goal, but it was thought that this goal could be better achieved gradually by methodical progress in carefully selected sectors. An experimental programme was accordingly put forward which was selective in two senses. 'First', said the report, 'it will give special attention to a small number of countries—not more than eight, chosen from among those which express willingness to take part in the programme. Secondly, it will concentrate on intensive experimental projects.'[2] Instead of attempting to teach literacy to all and sundry everywhere, the aim would be to single out sections of society where there was a strong incentive to learn, because literacy would help the learner to gain promotion or improve his business, and where the necessary opportunities were present 'for using education to raise the level of living and accelerate development'. By thus using the available resources in such a way as to eliminate waste as far as possible, and by closely relating literacy teaching to general educational,

81

social and economic development, it was felt not only that immediate results would be valuable, but that the experience gained and enthusiasm generated by the experimental programme would pave the way for an eventual world campaign against mass illiteracy.

The operational scheme required many months of planning, in consultation with the World Health Organisation, the Food and Agricultural Organisation and other official and unofficial international bodies concerned with social and economic development, and in negotiation with 'donor' and 'receiver' governments. Along with the general planning, steps would be taken, in consultation with the member states, to select the countries and projects to serve as experimental areas. Guidance was to be offered as to the criteria which should govern the selection process, and help would be given to those states which desired it in the preparation of projects for consideration. It was hoped that the necessarily lengthy procedure would allow for the choice of three countries for experiment by early 1966, three more during that year for action in 1967, and subsequently two more for action in 1968. The period for which projects would be assisted was envisaged as at least three years, and possibly up to five years and longer. First results should begin to appear from the third year onwards. It was hoped that these would enable the General Conference to consider at its meeting in 1970 the possibility of expansion of the experimental programme and even its extension into the long-awaited world campaign.

Between the circulation of this report and its consideration at the General Conference in November 1964 a further contribution to thought on the subject was made by a regional conference of the Arab states held at Alexandria in October 1964. This followed a summit conference of Arab kings and heads of state which, a month previously, had committed the Arab countries to joint action to eradicate illiteracy. The significance of such a conference in one of the world's most famous and ancient centres of culture was not lost on the delegates, who proudly claimed that the Arab peoples 'were the first to turn sign into symbol, symbol into script, and script into learning', and observed that Mohammed had prescribed that any captive who taught ten Muslims to read and write should be freed. Yet, despite considerable recent efforts to improve the situation, two-thirds of the peoples of the Arab world—nearly 50 million souls—remained illiterate, and this could not be tolerated.

The Alexandria conference therefore recommended that every Arab country should establish a plan to eradicate illiteracy within fifteen years; that the literacy campaign should be accorded its proper place in national plans for economic and social development (or be constituted as a special plan if no comprehensive development plan existed); and that a certain percentage of the national income should be earmarked for the education of illiterates. A specialised literacy agency should be set up to plan a pan-Arab literacy campaign, and to co-ordinate and assist the national efforts. A special Arab literacy fund should be set up and financed by contributions from the member states.[3] Here was ample evidence, if evidence were needed, that the problem of illiteracy was 'on the map'.

The General Conference of UNESCO, when it met in November 1964, fully approved 'unanimously and by acclamation' the Director-General's proposals for the experimental programme. It also accepted with gratitude an invitation from the Shahin-shah of Iran to organise, in Teheran, a World Congress of Ministers of Education on the Eradication of Illiteracy. This Congress was arranged to take place in September 1965. Meanwhile, the initial steps were taken to select the areas of experiment. In response to a circular enquiry, thirty-five countries* expressed the wish to submit projects for consideration, and a series of missions of experts (educators and economists) was sent out by UNESCO to help the countries concerned to draw up their plans. The 'brief' prepared for this purpose indicates the principles on which the new strategy was to be put into effect.

* More came forward later.

The first principle was that, as far as possible, all planning—and always the approval of plans—should be regarded as the responsibility of the government concerned. The role of the experts was to advise and give technical assistance. Secondly, while the aim was to prepare intensive experimental literacy projects, this should be done in the context of and in relation to the general development of the country. It was essential that literacy should not be regarded as an end in itself or illiteracy as a problem to be solved in isolation. Literacy, in fact, 'should be regarded as a necessary pre-investment measure for the creation and promotion of "human capital" as well as for the better use of physical capital'. Accordingly, projects should be 'functionally related' to high priority development.[4] This was a new conception, involving consideration of new teaching methods and media. A third important principle was that projects (which would always be projects of the government concerned, not of UNESCO or any other international organisation) must be concrete and definite. 'They must give full details about who is to be made literate, how and why.'[5] There must be no question of general assistance in this context to extensive nation-wide literacy campaigns. These would, however, continue to qualify for other assistance, whether multi-lateral or bilateral, under other schemes.

In preparation for the Teheran World Conference, UNESCO issued, among other documents, two papers of special importance: *Statistics of Illiteracy* and *Literacy as a Factor in Development*. Mention has already been made of the first. This, as the preamble explained, was prepared for the particular purpose of the Conference. *Statistics of Illiteracy* was not an up-to-date edition of the previous general surveys, being less complete in some respects and more fully detailed in others. It omitted reference to countries in which the illiteracy rate was estimated at less than 5 per cent, and a number of dependent territories (mostly islands) in which the rate was higher but the population very small. It also omitted, for want of the necessary material, mainland China. In all, ninety-six countries and territories were covered; in some cases the statistics now published were the first attempt at a detailed estimate of the number of illiterates. With a view to the specific objectives of the Teheran Conference, the tables for each country were as far as possible broken down according to sex, age groups, types of occupation and environment (urban or rural). Comparative figures were given, when available, for 1950 (or thereabouts) and 1962; also particulars of certain 'indicators'—the enrolment of primary school children, the annual increase in newsprint consumption, in the number of volumes in public libraries, in the number of radio receivers, in the national income and, finally, in the population. It was admitted that the estimation methods were often 'rather shaky', but at least the information provided valuable guidance as to current trends and future possibilities.

The broad conclusion to be drawn from the document was stated as follows:

> At present, the overall increase in the number of illiterates throughout the world over the last ten years and the general decline in the illiteracy rate during the same period would seem to show that the school enrolment effort alone, despite its tangible and sometimes spectacular results, is not at present succeeding on its own in stopping illiteracy by destroying it at the source. What is needed for some time to come, therefore, is a dual effort bearing simultaneously on school enrolment and adult education. Only by dint of that effort will illiteracy begin to show a marked decline.[6]

This statement gives a clear clue to what UNESCO hoped to gain from bringing ministers of education together in conference: a rethinking of conventional educational policy which would result in a move away from the traditional concentration on the formal education of the young to a new conception in which the claims of education for the older people would be recognised and budgetary provisions adjusted accordingly.

A similar consideration underlay the other pre-Conference paper, *Literacy as a Factor in Development*. The aim of this paper was modestly described as, 'on the basis of past experience, to indicate certain trends and to open up a number of avenues for thought and action'. Drawing attention to the 'enormous number' of adult illiterates and the 'extraordinarily high' illiteracy rate amongst women, the paper analysed the close connection between illiteracy and underdevelopment, of which illiteracy is both the cause and the effect. It proceeded to argue in some detail the case against there being any practical possibility of solving the problem by the extension of school attendance, leaving the adult illiterates 'to their fate, in vast and growing numbers, until the "species" dies out'. The 'disastrous consequences' of such a policy were set forth in grim detail—wastage of productive manpower, delay in social development, intergenerational conflict, acceptance of inferior status for women with all that this implies, and, finally, international disequilibrium and conflicts arising from the ever-widening gulf between countries with a high rate of illiteracy and those possessing advanced educational facilities.[7]

Governments came in for some criticism for past failure to give appropriate recognition to the importance of adult education—admittedly partly due to disillusionment caused by the poor results of some literacy campaigns which had been badly planned, provided with insufficient financial support, or inadequately followed up. Optimism, encouraged by the greatly increased interest taken by so many countries and peoples in the problem of illiteracy, was tempered by misgivings due to the too frequent neglect of 'taking account of all the prerequisites and, in particular, of the essential prerequisite of linking literacy with economic objectives'.[8]

The authors of *Literacy as a Factor in Development* then examined the relation between literacy and development. The existence of such a relationship was undoubted, but it was not necessarily a matter of cause and effect in the sense that an increase in literacy could be shown to have an automatic result in raising the *per capita* income of a community. The contribution which literacy could make to economic development depended upon the circumstances of the country concerned. It could be particularly significant in cases where development takes the form of industrialisation or the improvement of agricultural production. That literacy would have both direct and indirect effects on increasing productivity could safely be assumed, always provided that it was carried beyond the elementary stage and was progressively transformed into functional literacy. Otherwise, it might do as much harm as good by creating unsatisfied aspirations and might even prove to be a 'positively bad investment'.[9]

After further discussion along these lines and a statement of the case for the new selective approach, the document examined the question of the cost and financing of literacy teaching. It was found that costs varied so much from place to place, according to local circumstances, that no general conclusion could be offered. Further research on this aspect of the problem was needed. As for finance, the general principle emerging from past experience was that success depended upon fairly considerable financial effort by the state, and that literacy work warranted—and required—a greater financial effort on the part of governments than they had been willing to make hitherto. Whether the money should be charged to the education vote, or be specially provided, or be linked with development projects was a matter for each government to deal with according to the local circumstances. But in any case a 'reasonable proportion' of the national income should be earmarked for this work, and the funds made available should be increased as the national income grew. Along with such governmental provision, public and private undertakings, seeing that the teaching of literacy was a profitable investment for commerce and industry, might fairly be expected (and indeed strongly persuaded) to finance such teaching amongst their own employees. The value of voluntary assistance in cash and kind from religious bodies, trusts and individual benefactors was recognised. But when all was said and done, the countries concerned could not hope to solve their problems alone: outside aid through international co-operation was essential.[10]

Here again it was considered that hitherto international co-operation and assistance in the campaign against illiteracy, while by no means negligible, had fallen far short of that afforded in other fields of education. Moreover, the effect of the assistance given had all too often been disappointing owing to lack of a clear idea of the targets aimed at or of the nature and content of adult literacy programmes. Increased aid must be provided. It would not be 'gratuitous generosity' but the logical consequence of recognition that illiteracy is harmful to everyone. If it is allowed to persist, the countries affected cannot expand their consumption and production in the general interest of the economic development of all peoples, 'and the world will lack a potential heritage of civilisation that must remain almost inarticulate if the majority remains illiterate'.[11]

'The new message', this powerfully argued document concludes, 'that must be propagated is that this deep and many-sided relationship exists between literacy and development. To realise this and act accordingly may redound to the lasting honour of our times.'[12]

The world Congress (or Conference: both terms appear in the official documents) of Ministers of Education met in Teheran between September 8 and 19, 1965. It was attended by delegations (including thirty-seven ministers) from eighty-five member states, together with observers from the Vatican and a large number of official and unofficial organisations from many parts of the world. The secretariat was provided by UNESCO; the Iranian Minister of Education presided. The delegates approved UNESCO's selective strategy, expressed warm appreciation of the content of the paper *Literacy as a Factor in Development*, and accepted the concept of functional literacy, with the corollary that literacy teaching, while it must be integrated with a

88

country's educational programme, could no longer be viewed as a purely educational matter but was to an even greater extent bound up with general social, economic and cultural development and, as such, should have the support of the public as a whole.

Much importance was, therefore, attached to the mobilisation of public opinion by every available means; UNESCO would have a leading part to play in this essential prerequisite for success. In emphasising this point, the Congress went to the heart of the matter. After all, such an assembly of well-informed and responsible people could scarcely have failed to record its recognition that, in the world of the second half of the twentieth century, there are few if any countries or communities in which illiteracy is not a serious disadvantage; and that this not only directly affects the people concerned but indirectly affects everybody else. All would agree that something must be done about it, but it is when it comes to deciding who should do what that trouble begins. The countries in question have enormous difficulties which have to be met with resources that are all too slender; they reasonably expect to be helped by those who are better off. Those better-off countries have their difficulties too; there is never enough money to go round, for the luxury of yesterday becomes the necessity of today. It is asking a lot of taxpayers that they should agree to forgo things which they need, or at any rate want, in order that people far away may have some benefit. In public affairs charity certainly begins at home. Whenever in Britain, the United States or any other 'donor country' the national economy runs into difficulties, one of the first cries is to cut 'overseas aid'.

'Only an informed and enlightened public opinion can bridge the gap between resolutions and the facts of history, between words and deeds.'[13] So ran the report of the Congress, and a number of suggestions were made as to how such an opinion could be created, both in countries with a high rate of illiteracy and in those where the problems had been solved and the appeal must be made on the basis of international solidarity. Among other proposals was a recommendation that September 8, the date of the inauguration of the Congress, should be proclaimed as an annual World Literacy Day. The detailed conclusions and recommendations of the Congress ranged over the whole field of the subject: planning, organisation and research; recruitment and training of staff; provision of textbooks and reading materials and the use of audio-visual media; integration of the literacy campaign with the educational system and development plan of the country concerned; exchange of information and pooling of experience; co-operation amongst the developing countries and between those and the developed countries on a multilateral or bilateral basis; collaboration with unofficial and voluntary organisations; enlargement of UNESCO's programme and the provision by and through UNESCO of more substantial means than had hitherto been made available for the struggle against illiteracy.

So far as such a report could go, the results of the Congress were highly satisfactory to those who sought to see the problem of illiteracy firmly acknowledged as a primary issue of world concern. 'The unanimous acceptance', said the Director-General of UNESCO in his final comment on the proceedings, 'the unanimous acceptance—at any rate as working hypotheses—of a number of clear concepts was intellectually an inestimable gain. Striking unanimity had been reached regarding the practical approach in a debate in which realism had been the keynote. Such agreement between intellect and will made concerted action on a world scale feasible.' But he added: 'After the Congress would come the application, concerted action becoming, bluntly, action.'[14]

Only by the action which was to follow during the ensuing years could it be judged whether the Congress was in fact the turning point in the long story. All that one can say at the time of writing is that rapid progress was made in deciding on at least some of the projects to be brought under the scheme. Early in 1966, projects in Algeria, Iran and Mali were approved. The total cost of these was to be $12·8 million, of which $9 million was to be found by the countries concerned and the balance from the United Nations Development Programme. Later in the same year, projects in Tanzania and Ecuador were added to the list.

I shall deal with the wider implications of the Teheran report in my final chapter; here, however, is perhaps the most convenient place at which to note that, apart from the schemes of aid directly sponsored by UNESCO, a great variety of literacy programmes in many parts of the world is continually being undertaken by the governments concerned with financial and technical assistance provided, under bilateral arrangements, by one or other of the more affluent nations. The United States Agency for International Development (AID) has a massive organisation for giving such assistance, and a proportion of its activities is devoted to literacy, often in association with American universities and foundations. An excellent example of this is the Turkish Armed Forces Literacy Project which was started in 1959, after two years of planning, as a joint effort of the Turkish ministries of Defence and Education with the United States International Co-operation Administration (the forerunner of AID), assisted by a group from Georgetown University, Washington. It had been found that half the recruits entering the Turkish army were illiterate. Sixteen centres were established to which illiterate recruits were sent for two months' basic literacy instruction before going on to their military training. By 1961, between sixty and seventy thousand young men were passing through these courses every year.[15]

So far as Britain is concerned, the overseas aid organisation of the former Colonial Office, which used to administer the funds provided under the Colonial Development and Welfare Acts, was transferred in 1961 to the new Department of Technical Co-operation, which later became the Ministry of Overseas Development. The work of this ministry is mainly, but not exclusively, concerned with countries in the Commonwealth. It includes the support of literacy programmes by agreement with the local governments, within the limits of the resources available to it for this purpose. Somewhat similarly, the French government's official organisation for co-operation with developing countries deals mainly with those included in the Communauté Français; questions relating to literacy come within the purview of the Ministry of National Education.[16]

To attempt to assess what all this aid amounts to—in money, in technical help, in personnel—would involve much research; and probably, in view of the difficulty of separating literacy programmes from those concerned with community development or formal education, no very satisfactory result would be achieved. It must suffice to say that the help given under bilateral aid schemes is very substantial by any standard except the standard set by the immensity of the problem.

8

ORGANISATION OF LITERACY PROGRAMMES

IT WILL be clear from what has gone before that the subject of the organisation of literacy programmes is one with little more than a quarter of a century's study and experience behind it. It would be too much to say that a definitive pattern has now been worked out, and it may be doubtful whether such a pattern could be constructed, except in very general terms, since the circumstances vary greatly from place to place and from time to time. The form of a country's government is a major factor; the wealth or poverty of the country is another; the linguistic background yet another. An organisation devised for a predominantly urban community is unlikely to be suitable for a rural population, still less for one that is nomadic.

The experience so far gained in many parts of the world has been drawn upon in the compilation of one of UNESCO's invaluable manuals, published in 1966, on Adult and Youth Education: *The Planning and Organization of Adult Literacy Programmes in Africa*, by Peter du Sautoy of Manchester University. Although, as its title shows, this work is specifically related to the African continent, much of its contents is of general application, as indeed is to be expected, since tropical Africa itself covers a wide variety of local conditions, many of which have their parallels in other parts of the world. The manual ranges, in full detail and with great authority, over the whole field of the subject. Introductory chapters deal with basic principles, definitions and

93

motivation. There follows a practical guide to the planning process, the organisational structure, the financial issues involved, and the necessary publicity arrangements. Languages, teaching methods, materials and equipment, and the use of audio-visual aids are in turn discussed; and, finally, the recruitment, selection and training of instructors and supervisors, together with some observations on class-room techniques. I cannot attempt to do more here than to deal with the subject in a very general way, basing my remarks on this manual and other relevant sources.

One of the first questions that arises when a literacy campaign is contemplated is that of the language in which people are to be taught. It is rare, in the countries where illiteracy is rife, to find one language which is commonly spoken by the whole or even by the majority of the people who are to be made literate. There are good arguments to support the view that a person is most readily and effectively taught to read and write in his mother tongue, which may be the only one he knows. 'Use of the mother tongue for literacy instruction has the great advantage of simplicity and effectiveness', stated one of the commissions of the Teheran Congress. 'As the natural vehicle of the beginner's thought it facilitates the acquisition of knowledge, associates the new signs with known sounds and makes it unnecessary to learn a foreign vocabulary.'[1] It is clear that if, to the difficulties of learning to read and write, the difficulties of learning an alien language have to be added, the teaching of literacy must be slower, more expensive and less certain in its results than would otherwise be the case.

On the other hand, what is to be done where there is a multiplicity of mother tongues, sometimes varying almost from village to village, as in many parts of Asia and Africa? Some of them may well never have been reduced to writing at all, and a start has to be made by constructing an alphabet. Even where the written form already exists, there may well be no substantial quantity of literature available in it, apart, perhaps, from a

94

Gospel or a selection of Bible texts. Textbooks, primers, readers, follow-up material of all kinds have to be specially produced. Writers have to be trained. It all takes time and costs money; and at the end the newly literate person, though he may possess enough skill for elementary local needs, such as being able to read posters or instructional leaflets, has been given no key to open the gateway to knowledge in any broad sense of the word. Is the exercise really worth while? Is not any improvement in his lot merely marginal in comparison with the days when he relied upon the spoken word? If so, the question arises whether literacy should not always be taught, if not in an international language, such as English, French, Russian or Spanish, at least in a language which is in general use as a first or second language over a reasonably wide area (preferably the whole or the greater part of the country concerned, for community of language is a powerful force in consolidating national unity), and in which a considerable body of people is already literate and a fair quantity of literature of some sort is already available.

The answer clearly depends upon local circumstances. A possible compromise between the two extremes is to start by teaching the mother tongue and when the connection between sound, symbol and meaning has been established in the pupil's mind on the familiar ground, lead him on to learn to read and write in a more widely current language, such as the official language of his country. It is important, however, to bear in mind that the matter is not simply one of some authority deciding, on theoretical grounds, what would be 'best' for the illiterate person. The point of view of the person himself has to be considered. He may have his own strong opinion as to the language in which he wishes to be taught to read. Psychological and emotional factors are involved which cannot lightly be ignored, if the indispensable co-operation of the prospective pupil is to be secured. Political considerations, too, may have to be taken into account. There may be arguments for encouraging the use of a particular language in order to promote national unity or to strengthen

95

the country's ties to another country or group of countries. And in any case there are practical questions, which may be decisive, whatever the arguments: the availability of teachers, for instance; the existence or otherwise of established alphabets and orthographies in the languages from which the choice has to be made; the suitability of accepted scripts for reproduction by printing and typewriting; the extent to which reading matter is ready to hand or will have to be specially prepared, and, in the latter event, the possibility of finding writers capable of preparing it; and finally, not least important, the implications of all this for the cost of the campaign.

Decisions are unavoidably governed by such considerations as these; but it should not be overlooked that deeper issues are at stake. As was pointed out in a learned article in the *Times Literary Supplement* of November 10, 1966, the philosophic study of language in relation to human psychology and sociology has seen important developments during recent years, though it would appear that progress so far has consisted rather of opening up a wide field for research and speculation than of approaching any definite conclusions. What seems clear is that, inasmuch as the way of life of any community is profoundly influenced by and intimately bound up with the language used by the people, the choice of language for literacy teaching, especially if it involves immediate or gradual changes in the traditional language habits of the community concerned, may prove to have set in motion forces leading to consequences far outside the intentions or the vision of the contemporary planner.

To return to more mundane considerations: the experience of the earlier literacy campaigns described in previous chapters shows that, in any country where illiteracy presents a serious problem, it cannot practicably be tackled except at government level and with the full force of government machinery and money behind the effort. The attempts at literacy teaching undertaken before the Second World War by missionaries and other philanthropic bodies or individuals in India and elsewhere were doubtless of value to the limited numbers of persons immediately affected, and useful as pilot schemes for trying out teaching methods, but their impact on the problem of mass literacy was seldom significant. Some more, but not much, can be said of the later official schemes operated on a shoestring and in insufficient depth. In too many cases inadequate provision was made for those who had learned to read to derive some positive advantage from their effort, or for follow-up literature adequate in quality and in quantity to help them to progress from simple to functional literacy. There was no encouragement to them to form islands of literacy in a mainly illiterate population, and they soon relapsed into their former state.

Only the resources of government can suffice to mount a programme covering a wide enough area to be worth while and to furnish the services, in addition to the teaching itself, which are essential if the exercise is not to be a waste of time, money and effort. But what is a wide enough area? Various answers may be given to this question, but even the advocates of the selective approach are agreed that it is undesirable to think in terms of less than a whole community, forming 'an identifiable group with a precise geographical location and as homogeneous as possible',[2] which can be considered as a social unit and which is large enough to have a corporate way of life. Such a community might comprise all the inhabitants of a country or, failing that, the inhabitants of a province or a city, or even of the industrial quarter of a city, or the families concentrated in a particular area of agricultural development. The larger the unit is, the better, provided that the people concerned are consciously linked together by neighbourhood, shared interests or common loyalties. The leadership, the planning, and most of the money will, then, have to be provided by government, with or without external assistance. But, once it has been decided to embark on a literacy project, not only every department of the administration but every kind of social or voluntary organisation which is available must be brought into full participation, as well as the services of all individuals willing to give time and work to the cause.

One of the first questions asked is, very properly, what is it going to cost? It is easier to ask than to answer. The estimate prepared by UNESCO in 1963 assumed a cost of £2 to £3 a head. An attempt recently made in the Arab countries to estimate costs produced results varying from 80 cents to $61·80 per head; so wide a variation clearly indicates lack of uniformity in the factors brought into the calculation by different authorities, according, among other things, to whether the aim was seen as elementary literacy only, or as the provision of a full programme of functional literacy and adult education. In some countries it has been considered that the unit cost of one year of literacy teaching is comparable to that of one year of primary schooling. Much more research is needed and is being vigorously conducted. What can be asserted with confidence is 'that the cost of educating an adult is considerably less than that of educating a child, and that a literate adult is more immediately productive. This is one reason for regarding the financing of adult education as a very satisfactory investment of capital.'[3]

When government has made the basic decisions—who are to be taught and in what language or languages—when it has ensured the necessary budgetary provision, and has negotiated any financial or technical assistance needed from outside, it is axiomatic that the direction of the programme should be vested in a single executive authority armed with requisite powers. The form which this authority should take will vary with local circumstances. In some cases it may be appropriate to set up a special ministry or department; in others existing machinery may be used, with provision for co-ordinating the various aspects of official and unofficial effort. The essential point is that the importance of the work, and the necessity to avoid waste of labour and resources, should be recognised by giving the responsible authority a place in the government structure which is high enough to secure the co-operation, at all levels, of the many departments and bodies concerned at different points in the general scheme of operations.

The staffing of a literacy project is a matter to which much thought has naturally been given. A basic question is whether to make use of the members of the local teaching profession or to recruit a special staff for the purpose. There are arguments both ways, and the views and experience of governments and practitioners vary. The considerations which have to be taken into account are ably stated by Professor A. S. M. Hely, of Adelaide University, in a manual—*The School Teacher and Adult Education* —published by UNESCO in 1966. Teachers are, after all, trained to teach; and primary school teachers, who form the largest part of the profession, are in particular trained to teach reading. They are familiar with the local language, the social conditions and the people, many of whom are the parents of their pupils. It is to the advantage of their professional work that the children they have taught should not return to illiterate backgrounds and lose the effect of their schooling. Moreover, if it is agreed that the teaching of literacy to adults should be placed in the context of a general programme of adult education, it is clear that the professional teacher, as one of the small minority of the population acquainted with educational principles and practices, must have a significant part to play in that programme, and should be concerned with the literacy aspect of the programme as well as with the rest.

On the other hand, there are those who hold that the employment of professional school teachers for adult literacy instruction is positively undesirable in principle. It is pointed out that the professional teachers are already far too few (even in countries like Britain) to cope with the educational needs of the ever growing child population. They have quite enough on their plate if they are to do their normal work properly, without being burdened by additional tasks. 'If they have done their work conscientiously during the day', wrote Dr Laubach, 'they are too tired to show the consideration and the enthusiasm tired adults will require. For good results one should not teach adults when one is weary. . . . Any teacher who teaches until midnight will make a poor job of teaching the children the following morning!'[4] Further, the training and techniques of primary school teachers are specifically directed towards the education of young children. The school teacher is accustomed to discipline his pupils, to punish them if they do not work hard or pay attention, to have what he says accepted without question. He will not find it easy to adapt himself to the entirely different attitude demanded of him by an adult class. 'An illiterate adult', wrote Mallam Ahmadu Coomassie in the paper from which I have already quoted, 'is unlike a child in many respects. He is filled with experiences, both negative and positive. . . . He may be handicapped because of lack of literacy and therefore may wish to attend a literacy class. But he will continue to come only if he learns something which seems of immediate and practical use to him.'[5] He will certainly not stay if the teacher, who may be of no greater intelligence or status than himself, attempts to deal with him in a condescending or hectoring manner.

For these reasons, school teachers were deliberately not employed in the Nigerian campaign with which Mallam Ahmadu Coomassie was concerned. In most cases, however, a compromise solution has been found most satisfactory. The scarcity of professional teachers alone would preclude reliance on them for giving the elementary instruction in a mass literacy programme. The general experience gained over the years shows, however, that direct instruction at that stage can be and is probably best done by an army of volunteers who have undergone a very simple form of training designed purely to enable them to impart to others the elements of literacy. They do not necessarily have to be 'educated' people; in the Northern Nigerian campaign, the best instructors were found amongst those who had themselves but recently taken the literacy course. But if they have some general education, so much the better. This does not mean that the professional teacher should be left out of the programme. On the contrary, his services are greatly needed: for training the instructors, for supervising the field work, and for the follow-up. Recognising this, some governments have begun to include study of the requirements and techniques of adult education and community development in the normal curricula of the teacher training institutions.

One or two examples may be cited to illustrate the variety of the expedients which have been devised to suit the needs of particular national circumstances. In Ethiopia, the National Literacy Campaign organisation, which was inaugurated in July 1962, under the patronage of the Emperor Haile Selassie, was a voluntary movement aimed at giving instruction to the whole people, irrespective of age, sex, religion or occupation, in the reading and writing of Amharic. At the start, the organisation recruited numbers of secondary school students as volunteer instructors and provided them with short training courses. As the work developed, experienced school teachers were brought in to act as part-time field supervisors, whose task was to organise new centres and stimulate interest in the country districts. In the Cuban campaign of 1961 the professional teachers performed a similar role.

An experiment of an original kind was undertaken in Iran in 1962, when it was decided to establish an 'Army of Knowledge'. Under this plan, youths who have completed secondary education and are due for eighteen months' military service can be exempted from that service and drafted instead into a 'literacy corps'. Those selected for this assignment receive intensive training in barracks, after which they are sent out to rural areas to start schools. The main effort here is directed at teaching the children, only about half of whom were able to go to school at the time when the scheme was initiated; but the idea of using a disciplined service in this way is clearly one worth consideration in connection with adult teaching in countries where suitable arrangements exist. It was, in fact, commended to the attention of the governments concerned by the Teheran Conference of 1965.[6]

One point which may have to be taken into account is the possible reluctance of adults to submit to instruction by very young people, unless the latter are carefully trained to offer their services with due modesty and to show proper respect to their seniors. It is not as if one can assume that illiterate adults are invariably eager to learn to read and write at any price. The very fact that they are illiterate often prevents them from realising what they are missing on account of their illiteracy. The more limited a person's mental horizon is, the more he is likely to be conservative and suspicious of anything calculated to disturb the precarious balance of his adjustment to the needs and problems of daily life. The first necessity in any literacy campaign is to sell the product to the customer; and this means securing his confidence. In the planning of modern literacy programmes, great attention is therefore paid to this essential question of 'motivation'. Mention has already been made of the intensive propaganda carried out by the Soviet government in order to secure the co-operation of the people in its great literacy drive. In that case use could be and was made of both negative and positive incentives: social disgrace for failure to co-operate, and advantages to be gained by compliance. The second kind of incentive is probably the more powerful and is certainly more commonly available to the promoters of a campaign.

'The history of literacy movements throughout the world is full of the debris of failures, chiefly because the classes were started without creating a strong desire or motivation among the students for learning to read or write'. This extract from an official Indian handbook is quoted in *ABC of Literacy* by Mary Burnet, who gives a number of instances of factors influencing people against learning to read and write. Superstition can be an obstacle: so may religious or racial prejudices. Some people are sceptical and need to be convinced that literacy will really be of any use to them. Some are genuinely disturbed about the possible effects on their way of life. 'One teacher', says Mary Burnet, 'trying to get men in a North African town to let their wives attend classes, said to one of them: "If your wife would come, she could learn how to write letters." "To whom?" asked the husband, bristling.'[7] Dr Laubach quotes the objection raised by a Moro chief who rejoiced in ten wives: 'I don't want my wives to be educated. Nobody could live with several educated wives; they would talk too much.'[8]

In the Northern Nigeria campaign referred to in Chapter 5, one young lady hit on a novel and effective kind of incentive. When approached by a man, she produced a notebook and pencil and invited him to write down his name. Only those who were able to do so qualified for her favours. More seriously, in the preparation of the public for that campaign, considerable stress was laid on the disadvantageous position of the illiterate person in a society in which taxes have to be paid and regulations observed, so that there are unlimited opportunities for unscrupulous literates to cheat their ignorant brethren. The same point has been made in other campaigns; for example, in this appeal of 1938 by the General Manager of the Tata Iron and Steel Company to the workers in Jamshedpur, Bihar, India: 'I have known of numerous instances in which your ignorance has been exploited by unscrupulous moneylenders and you have been prevailed upon to sign promissory notes for amounts far in excess of what you actually borrowed. . . . It is only with the growth of literacy amongst you that you will be able to minimise the evil of indebtedness.'[9] It was in this Bihar campaign that, 'young boys went to towns and villages singing rousing songs about the value of being literate, and ending each verse with the refrain "Each one teach ten".' In the Indian state of Aundh, at about the same time, 'the Rajkumar himself took a leading part in the campaign, going with his Rani from village to village, and singing *Kirtans* on literacy.'[10]

Modern developments have put more effective weapons at the disposal of literacy programme organisers. Transport from place to place is easier and more ground can be covered than in the old days of foot safari. Radio, cinema vans, film strips, television and tape recording ease the task of communication. Techniques and procedures must clearly be adapted to the local circumstances; but it remains generally true that the organisation of any literacy campaign is not simply a matter of providing teaching staff and teaching material and of opening classes. All this is useless unless it is accompanied by a planned and intensive effort, based on careful research into local customs and conditions, to arouse the interest and enthusiasm of the people who are to be taught.

'It is never too late to learn! It is never too late to learn!' bellows a voice through the loudspeaker mounted in the shiny white truck, as the driver zigzags through the confusion of housewives, children and chickens in the village street. The housewives stare. The chickens squawk as they flutter out of the way. The children, delighted with anything new, run shouting after the truck as it rolls on towards the one-room school house.

The driver jumps out with a poster in one hand and a paste-pot in the other. A few minutes later, any villager who does know how to read can explain again to his neighbour what the loudspeaker has already announced. Classes for grown-ups are going to be started. The next night people will come to show pictures and answer questions, and after that any man or woman who wants to can give his name to the teacher and start going to this new kind of school.[11]

In these vivid sentences Mary Burnet has described the end-product of all the international and governmental planning, the philosophising and technical argument, the search for money and staff, the patient building up of an organisation—all this in order that literacy may come to a village of Africa, or India, or South America, or wherever men and women need, even if they do not realise it, to be able to read and write if they are to make terms at all with life as it has to be lived in these days.

But the end is only the beginning. As has already been observed, it is futile to organise a literacy programme merely for the purpose of teaching. That purpose calls for the production and use of primers and textbooks, but a programme which provides nothing more than these for the new reader is foredoomed to failure. It is no use to leave the provision of 'follow-up' literature to a later stage. Its planning and production must be considered as an integral and essential part of the campaign, and no stretch of imagination is needed to see how very greatly this adds to the difficulty, complexity and cost of organising a campaign. Given the will and the money, teachers can be found. Enough experience of teaching has now been gained to establish technical principles which it is not too difficult to apply to given local situations. The teachers will not lack for students if the advantages of literacy are sufficiently publicised. But unless the students find things to read which are intelligible, useful and attractive, they will quickly give up, and others will not even trouble to make a start.

Yet the provision of such reading material presents a problem in itself of such magnitude as almost to overshadow the problem of organising the teaching of literacy. The publications have to be numerous and varied enough to sustain interest. They have to deal with matters which are relevant to the daily life of the people concerned. They have to be graded in vocabulary and syntax so that readers may progress from the simple to the more sophisticated as their reading ability develops. And at all levels they must be couched in adult, not childish, terms. As a general rule, such literature can only be satisfactorily produced by local writers familiar with the thought-processes and idioms of the people. Rarely, however, are such writers available in the kind of community for which a literacy campaign is needed. Suitable persons have to be discovered and trained: no easy matter in any circumstances, but particularly difficult when a highly specialised kind of writing is called for. All this takes time as well as money; but it is fundamental to the organisation of a successful literacy programme and must be planned for from the outset.

Nor is it of any use to produce the follow-up literature unless it can be got into the readers' hands. It must be provided in sufficient numbers. It has to be transported and distributed, probably over a wide area of scattered villages and settlements linked by poor communications. It has to be made available free of charge, or at any rate at a nominal price which is unlikely to bear any relation to the cost of production and distribution.

These aspects of the problem will be discussed in more detail in subsequent chapters; but first it will be convenient to consider the special technical questions that arise in connection with the actual teaching.

9

TEACHING PEOPLE TO READ

THERE IS no one universally accepted method which applies to all the varying conditions in which literacy may have to be taught. But there are general principles of teaching adult illiterates, and although much has happened since Laubach first endeavoured to formulate these principles, his observations on the subject in *India Shall Be Literate* are still valid.

We have no *final* method yet, excepting to be forever dissatisfied, to beware of adhering too closely to any one theory or authority, to study all methods, to try those that look most promising, to adopt what is best, to improve on them where possible, and to throw them away the moment something better appears. . . . There are those who say that several methods are equally good and that 'the will to learn is what really matters'. This simply is not the whole truth nor half of the truth. Easy lessons with interesting content will beget the will to learn, while over-difficult lessons with no meaning will discourage the stoutest heart.[1]

Laubach sets forth the prescription for an ideal set of lessons thus:

1. *Learnability:* the lessons will be   absorbingly interesting
easy
swift

2. *Teachability:* the lessons can be

                                    taught by anybody
taught as soon as learned
partly self-taught without a teacher present

The teacher, he says, 'must treat his adult student not like a child or an inferior, but as politely as he would treat a high official.'

The slightest suggestion that the teacher feels superior will ruin the teaching. For the illiterate adult is extremely sensitive. He suffers from a sense of inferiority. Even when he boasts and swaggers, he is revealing an 'inferiority complex'— which means that he tries by bombast to hide from himself and others his real feeling of insignificance.

It is exceedingly easy to discourage the illiterate. . . . Give him a compliment instead of a correction! Treat him like a raja!

. . . If an illiterate adult is made unhappy for one minute he will get up and leave your class, and denounce literacy to everybody he meets. He can be kept studying only if he is happy and encouraged. What everybody in this world loves most is somebody who will discover an unsuspected diamond in him. The illiterate, paralyzed with despair, if you tell him how bright he really is, tingles from head to foot.

. . . Never teach a man if you do not like him. The illiterate cannot read books but he does read human nature, and he knows in a second whether your smile reveals real brotherly interest. . . . Personally I try always to pray for my student. . . .

Some people would teach better if they were handcuffed.

Do not waste a second or a word. The first fifteen minutes are the most precious with adults.

Resist the temptation to indulge in a speech before the lesson.

Adults want progress, the faster the better, as long as it is easy.

Keep out of the adult's way . . . . Almost every illiterate recognises a few letters and some illiterates know all the letters without being able to read words. You must neither hold the student back nor push him faster than he wishes to go.

Do not tell him what he already knows. Do not ask him any question he cannot answer. There must be no tests or examinations.

Never ask a question twice. Tell the student at once if he hesitates to answer.[2]

These quotations and other similar admonitions illustrate the fundamental difference between the teaching of children in school and the teaching of literacy to adults. The school teacher is employed, not by the pupil, but by some authority—family or government—who wants something done to and for the child. His job is not merely to impart facts and skills, but to train the child's mind, to develop his character by discipline and competition, to make him work for his own good. The teacher of adults has to forget all that and remember that, whoever employs or pays him, he is in effect the servant, not the master, of his pupil. The pupil may well be his equal or superior in everything but literacy, and his sole responsibility towards the pupil is to enable him to read and write as quickly and easily as possible. It is no business of his to impose penalties for failure to learn, or to make the inapt pupil appear ridiculous.

So much for the teacher's approach to his task. Next we must consider the tools with which he has to work. The first need, obviously, is an alphabet, and if one does not exist for the language to be taught, it must be invented, or, more probably, borrowed or adapted from a suitable existing model. In practice, the alphabet to be used has usually been chosen, or established by local custom, long before the commencement of a literacy programme, and the teacher has to take things as he finds them. The teaching techniques to be employed, and the ease or difficulty of the instructor's and student's tasks are considerably affected by the alphabet which will be used. Different alphabets have their own special advantages and disadvantages for particular languages, and much depends on the extent to which the chosen alphabet effectively and consistently reproduces the sounds of the spoken word.

Given the alphabet, the next need is to compile a basic word list. The purpose of this is to identify the words that the learner will most easily be taught to recognise and memorise. This may seem a simple matter, but in fact the preparation of such a list is a long and difficult task, involving much research and local knowledge. It is not rendered easier by the fact that common usage may often vary from village to village; and, oddly enough, it is in regard to the most familiar things of life that variations are especially liable to occur.

When the word lists have been settled, and any queries about spelling satisfactorily disposed of, the way is clear to construct a primer. 'A primer is a teaching aid in the form of one or more books or booklets which is used during the basic stage of learning to read and write.' 'The function of the primer is that each one of its sheets or groups of sheets means a step in learning to recognise printed symbols for their meaning.' 'It is the pupil's "handbook" and the teacher's main instrument; it is at the same time a guide, a fixed depository of knowledge and a timetable for learning and teaching.'[3] These quotations are taken from a most valuable UNESCO handbook by Karel Neijs on the construction, evaluation and use of literacy primers. This book assembles the information and evidence afforded by the experience of literacy organisers and teachers in many parts of the world, sets forth the general principles involved and makes suggestions to help those who approach the problem for the first time. There is a wealth of detail, from which I can only attempt here to single out some of the salient points.

There can be no standard blueprint for the compilation of

primers, for there are too many variable factors. Languages and alphabets differ, and so do the relations of the former to the latter, so that in some cases teaching may best begin with letters; in others with syllables or even with whole words. The general cultural level of the community concerned is an important factor: so is the level of education and intelligence of the prospective instructors or teachers. It is generally agreed that a literacy course should be conceived in three or four stages, each self-contained. 'Adults might hesitate to start on a long period of training but be quite willing to register for the first stage which aims at reaching simple reading activities in a relatively short period of time. Once their interest is caught they can be persuaded to stay on.'[4] The kind of arrangement is:

Stage 1—preparatory, aimed at arousing interest and introducing the student to the idea of connecting symbols with sounds and meanings.

Stage 2—basic literacy, aimed at enabling the student to read a small selected vocabulary (200 to 400 words) and to begin practice in writing and simple arithmetic.

Stage 3 and subsequent—towards functional literacy, enabling the student to progress to the use of reading and writing in daily life.

The primer is concerned with the second stage. Its main function is to be a teaching aid. Whether it should attempt to convey information or ideas at the elementary stage is a question on which opinions differ; but at any rate it is clearly desirable that its subject matter, however simple, should be such as to engage the interest and attention of the learner. Its actual content depends on the teaching method which it has been decided to employ in the particular case. This is a highly technical question, and I cannot presume here to do more than indicate some of the considerations that arise. A full and valuable discussion of the various possible methods is contained in *The Teaching of Reading and Writing: an International Survey*, by W. S. Gray, and a summary will be found in Peter du Sautoy's manual referred to in the previous chapter.

Broadly speaking, there are two kinds of method used in teaching literacy to adults, and there are arguments for and against each in the context of particular languages. The kind of method which has been longest established and in the past most widely used is based on the recognition of the letters of the alphabet and of the sounds associated with them; this may be extended by presenting the learner with combinations of letters to form syllables, and from that he proceeds to words. This 'synthetic' method is best suited to phonetic languages, that is to say, those in which letters consistently stand for the same sounds. It is less suitable for languages (such as English) in which the same letter or combination of letters may signify more than one sound. A general disadvantage of this type of method is that it involves a good deal of mechanical memorisation which adults are liable to find difficult and boring.

The other kind of method is based not on sound but on meaning. At the start, the learner is shown a word and told what it is, so that he associates its visual form with the word as spoken and understood. Some authorities even prefer to begin with simple phrases or sentences containing a few words. It has been found that this type of method is more interesting to the adult and leads more quickly to intelligent reading, always provided that care is taken at every stage to ensure that the learner is made to understand how the word is to be analysed into the letters and syllables which combine to produce it A further development of this method is the 'story' technique, in which the words and sentences used in successive lessons are connected so as to make up a story on some subject which is of interest to the learner. While this 'global' method has evident attractions, it has been criticised on the grounds of its putting too much strain on the pupil, and of its needing the guidance of a more skilled teacher than may usually be available.

Both kinds of method have their advocates, but in the most

modern practice there is apparent a tendency towards what Professor Gray has called the 'eclectic system'. This consists of combining the elements of the different methods in the way best suited to the language and the circumstances of the programme concerned. Often it has been found desirable to carry out controlled experiments in the field before settling on a definite pattern. The quality of the prospective teachers, the facilities for training them, the capacities of the people to be taught and the time they can give to learning are amongst the factors which have to be taken into account.

Whatever teaching method is adopted, the form of the primers and other teaching material will depend upon it. If, as in most of the earlier primers, many of which remain in current use, the chosen starting point is the letter, the initial lessons will be devoted to the recognition of selected letters, introduced either individually or as parts of syllables or short words. As soon as any letters have been mastered, whether singly or in combinations, they are presented in actual use in selected 'key words', which are accompanied by an appropriate illustration, and these words are then quickly shown as grouped phrases and sentences. Thus a Javanese primer deals on its first page with the letters A, M, N and T. The vowel is at the top of the page. Below it are four columns: the left-hand column is a series of pictures; the next shows the consonants individually; in the third they are combined with the vowel into syllables (MA, NA, TA), in the fourth column into words (MAMA, ANA and so on) and phrases of two or three words. The same procedure is repeated in subsequent lessons, introducing new letters and combinations at each stage.

Much importance is attached to the key-word system, which was developed by Laubach in the Philippines. Key words are concrete nouns or action verbs chosen for their suitability to what the lesson is about, which may be one or more letters or syllables, or the word itself. As well as the key words, use is made of 'sight words', being those so common that the student should learn to recognise them at sight, whether or not they have any teaching value. In the Niger programme, the students were taught in the first lesson to read and write the name of their village and the word 'Niger'.[5]

After a few lessons along these lines, the learner can move on to sentences and stories, elementary at first, but progressively more complicated. In this way he comes to appreciate the connection between symbols and meaning, and the relevance of reading to practical life. Interest can be stimulated and useful information can be imparted which will help him along the way to functional literacy.

If, on the other hand, the so-called 'global' method has been adopted, the primer will probably take the form of a connected story, beginning with a sentence or two on the first page and going forward from that point, page by page, in a carefully graded progression. In this case, letter and word recognition will be practised by the use of cards and other supplementary visual material with which the instructor will have been supplied.

Instruction in writing is usually introduced at a very early stage of the course, with preparatory exercises leading to copying the letters and words seen in the primer. Figures, and their use in simple arithmetic, are also customarily taught at the primer stage of a literacy course, whether this instruction is included in the primer itself or made the subject of a separate booklet.

Enough has been said to show that, although simplicity is of the essence of a primer, for that very reason the construction of a primer is far from being a quick or easy job. Simplicity combined with effectiveness is the hardest thing to achieve in any connection. Ideally, as Neijs's UNESCO handbook points out, the compilation of a primer involves the co-operation of a number of highly expert specialists: adult education workers with local knowledge and experience, linguists, psychologists, experienced teachers, expert writers, illustrators competent in this field and typographers. The ideal is not always attainable, but long and careful preparation and experiment are necessary and the work of preparing a single primer may well take a year or more.

Many primers produced with the best intentions have failed
in their object because they were found confusing and difficult
by the learners, usually on account of their attempting to convey
too much at a time. Others have failed because they were boring, not enough care having been taken to ensure that the
contents and illustrations would arouse the readers' interest.
Many, too, have failed on account of bad layout or production,
poor illustrations or none. 'An attractively produced primer
invites learning. A book often is a new and strange thing to illiterates; let it be to them an object pleasant to handle and to
look at.'[6]

A primer may be in one or more volumes. To some extent,
this depends on the language and the length of the alphabet;
but on the whole, though there is some convenience and economy in bringing everything within one cover, the balance of
advantage would seem to lie in division into a series of smaller
booklets. This helps to give the learner a sense of achievement as
he progresses from book to book. The smaller volumes are convenient to handle or put in the pocket and accidental losses are
more easily made good.

It is fatal to the success of a primer to attempt to economise on
space. Only one very simple lesson can be placed on a page;
type must be large, room must be provided for illustrations
which may well occupy anything from a quarter to half of the
area covered; and plenty of blank space must be left to rest the
reader's eye. A complete primer may run to, say, 120 pages—or
rather three booklets averaging 40 pages each. An Urdu primer
which has become established in rural areas of West Pakistan
deals with a rather complicated language situation in three
books. The first (31 pages) introduces in the four initial lessons
15 letters and 17 words. After revision of what has been learned
so far, four further lessons introduce 9 more letters and 29 more
words. The second book (38 pages) likewise falls into two sections: four lessons introduce 13 letters and other symbols and 51

words, and after revision four more lessons introduce 6 letters and symbols and 50 words. In the third book (52 pages) seven reading lessons introduce 90 words; counting and writing are also introduced. Four more reading lessons followed by a folk-story complete the primer by adding 140 words to the learner's equipment. A simpler kind of primer, using the Roman alphabet and one supplementary symbol, in the Lugbara language of West Nile, included 39 lessons in 28 pages. The first 26 lessons each introduce one letter, and in the remaining 13, consonant clusters and the additional symbol are brought in with words and sentences. This short primer does not, however, provide for revision or supplementary reading material.

Particular attention has to be paid to illustrations, which are essential to the teaching method. Colour is helpful where practicable and is almost a 'must' for the cover. Line drawings are usually to be preferred to reproduced photographs, but the design of line illustrations for this purpose is a specialised business. These pictures must be well drawn, kept strictly to the point without extraneous detail and convey their meaning with absolute clarity. Experience has shown that it is very necessary to pre-test the drawings by showing them to the kind of people for whom the primer is intended, before they are committed to the printer. A drawing which looks quite in order to a sophisticated viewer may convey to a person not accustomed to look at pictures a meaning quite different from what is intended. Another UNESCO manual, *Simple Reading Material for Adults: Its Preparation and Use* (to which I shall be referring later), gives some examples. In one drawing a bridge was seen as a house; in another the door of a hut was thought to be a bed, and a background of distant hills was thought to be a clothes-line. Again, prospective learners can easily be put off if they are shown something which they consider impossible or ridiculous: people wearing the wrong sort of clothes or doing something which is contrary to local custom. As fashions and habits may vary greatly within a small area, the task of the illustrator is full of pitfalls.

The primer is the instructor's principal and indispensable tool; but modern developments have added some supplementary aids to lighten his task. Radio has been used with some effect in Malaya and elsewhere, and television has been tested where it is available, but on the whole the more complicated audio-visual gadgets are irrelevant for the present purpose. There are, however, several devices which are suitable and indeed indispensable for the amateur teacher. The most common and obvious is the blackboard. Film strips are useful when projectors are available. 'Flash cards' displaying single letters, syllables or words are much used. Ideally there should be one for every word in the primer. They are held up to the class for 'recognition drill', the exposure being shortened as proficiency is acquired. Other sets of cards are given out to the learners to arrange in words or sentences.

Charts are of great assistance to the instructor. These may conveniently be much enlarged reproductions of selected pages from the primer, which can be pinned up on the wall or blackboard. The 'flannelgraph'* is another device very useful in literacy teaching, and lends itself to word and letter games which combine instruction with entertainment. A 'wall newspaper' or news bulletin, using the vocabulary reached in the class's current study of the primer, is excellent not only for stimulating interest and giving practice in reading, but for conveying information and ideas. It is extensively used in China, amongst other places. Untrained teachers do not, however, find it easy to compose suitable material in this form, and it is best done by a central authority and distributed to the field instructors.

Directions for the use of the primer and the supplementary teaching aids, together with general guidance about teaching

* The flannelgraph 'consists of a piece of rough towel or flannel stretched on a wall or board; flash cards or cut-out pictures with a small square of flannel or sandpaper on the back will stick to this, enabling the learners as well as the teachers to practise making words and sentences, and to use the flannelgraph as a visual aid. There are variations on this technique, using plastic or metal and magnets, to make the pictures adhere to the board."

methods and detailed instructions for the conduct of lessons, the keeping of records and so on, are usually contained in a separate teachers' manual, which will include specific examples of lessons and illustrations demonstrating the techniques.

There is no standard length for a literacy course. Many variable factors have to be taken into account: the degree of proficiency aimed at, the number and capability of the available instructors, the previous background of the learners, the relative intelligence of individuals and the time which they can spare for attending classes. Some languages can be taught in fewer lessons than others. A very tentative estimate, given in Neijs's UNESCO handbook, is that the preparatory (pre-primer) stage may need from four to eight lessons, and the primer stage anything from forty to a hundred. After that it may take as many as 200 lessons to bring the student to the point of functional literacy. It has been said that an illiterate person can be taught to read in six weeks, and this would seem to be a fair guess, assuming that the language is one with which he is already familiar in its spoken form, that he or she can attend lessons more or less daily, and that conditions are generally favourable. The basic literacy course for Turkish army recruits lasts less than two months; but these students are receiving practically full-time instruction and their position is very different from that of civilians who can only give, perhaps, an hour in the evenings when the day's work is done. In Cuba, the average length of the course was two to three months. In some countries of Latin America, the duration has been fixed at six months. So, too, in Thailand and Vietnam. In these cases, however, the course has included some general subjects as well as literacy pure and simple.

What is clear is that any course of, say, three months or less, even if it is concentrated on literacy, cannot carry the learner beyond the stage of what is technically termed 'neo-literacy'. To do this and no more is a waste of money and effort. He must be enabled to develop and use his new skill; otherwise all experience shows that he will quickly lose interest and sooner rather than later relapse into illiteracy. Follow-up is essential. To a large extent it is a matter of making available and accessible to him a supply of suitable and useful reading material; but during the period of transition towards functional literacy he will almost certainly need help and guidance, and a literacy programme should include provision for this for anything from six months to a year after the conclusion of the primary course. This goes beyond the scope of the routine lesson which can be taught by amateur teachers, and merges into the field of adult education in the broader sense.

10

READING MATERIAL FOR NEW
READERS

'WHETHER LITERACY is really an important contribution to
the lives of a people or not depends upon the material that the
people read after they become literate. At least one-half of the
literacy problem, therefore, is what to provide for new literates
to read, in the transition period while they are building up a
vocabulary to the level where they can easily read and enjoy
standard literature.'[1]

So wrote Dr Laubach in 1947. The point which he makes is
less obvious than might appear at first sight. Once anyone has
grasped the principle of connecting visual symbols with sounds
and meanings, progress forward from that stage of basic literacy
is a matter of practice and opportunity. No further instruction is
really needed, anyhow not the kind of instruction which, as during the basic stage, can be given by an amateur teacher working
to a simple set of rules. There is, however, a large gap between
the vocabulary used by a person who has only known a spoken
language and that used in any ordinary book or newspaper. In
order to gain real benefit from literacy, the new literate has to
learn not only the appearance and spelling but the meaning and
pronunciation of a whole lot of words which are quite new. The
natural solution to this problem is to provide him with a graduated series of reading matter which he finds interesting and
valuable in itself and which continually introduces him to new
words until he has accumulated a full vocabulary. It does not
take much imagination to see that this is a formidable operation,

and it is only in the second half of this century that real attempts have been made to come to grips with it. For long it was assumed that the teaching of people to read would of itself create a demand for literature, and that demand would in the ordinary course of events attract supply. Such thinking is natural to people accustomed to a way of life in which education and publishing have developed together over the years, so that children pass on, in the course of their schooling, from simple to more complex books and arrive at the adult stage fully literate and providing a market for the commercial publisher; but it is inapplicable to the developing country, and to this illusion is largely due the fact that, in the trenchant phrase of a UNESCO document: 'literacy campaigns have earned more tombstones than monuments'.[2]

Let us consider for a moment what is involved. In the first place, the literature to be provided for the neo-literate has to be methodically planned, not only as regards form and content but as regards the vocabulary to be employed, the choice of new words to be introduced and the stages by which they are successively introduced. This can only be done as the result of patient and exhaustive research. Second, the literature must be attractive to the potential reader. The subjects must be such as interest him—closely related to his everyday problems or offering him the kind of entertainment which he appreciates. The presentation must be such as to make him want the book and, having obtained it, want to finish it. This again calls for much research and testing out before, during and after production, as well as for special skill on the part of writer, illustrator and printer. Third, the literature has to be accessible to the reader. Sufficient quantities have to be produced, and made available to the reader at the time when he wants them. And they cost money. The reader will not take them if he has to pay more than he thinks he can afford, or possibly if he has to pay for them at all. It is quite safe to assume that he will not in any case be able or willing to pay anything like an economic price.

It is obvious that these requirements cannot be met by private enterprise. A considerable organisation is needed which has to be heavily subsidised from some source.

The Christian missionaries who pioneered so many of the early literacy campaigns were chiefly concerned that people should be put in a position to read the Scriptures for the benefit of their spiritual welfare. The massive operations inaugurated in the nineteenth century by the British and Foreign Bible Society, and supplemented by the work of the American and other national Bible societies, aimed at making it possible for everyone in the world eventually to have access to the Scriptures in his own language and at a price which he could afford. Today these societies are circulating the Scriptures, in whole or in part, at a rate of well over 50 million new copies a year in some 1,200 different languages. The work is subsidised by the money which the societies collect from well-wishers in the donor countries. While the greater part of the distribution is carried out by the churches themselves in the countries concerned, there is a good deal of selling directly to the public, especially in remoter areas, by itinerant vendors known in Bible society parlance as colporteurs.

By its constitution the British and Foreign Bible Society was precluded from adding any note or comment to the bare text, and until recently from publishing less than a full book of the Bible (for example a Gospel). While there is plenty of evidence that these publications are eagerly read by those into whose hands they come, no one could claim that the Biblical writings are easy or simple for the unassisted reader. Other religious societies have therefore been formed for publishing and distributing ancillary Christian literature to suit various levels of educational attainment and degrees of literacy. Among others, the Society for Promoting Christian Knowledge and the United Society for Christian Literature are old-established British bodies active in the field of publication and distribution.

The most devout believer would not, however, claim that the needs of a man can be fully met by the Scriptures or by religious publications. Such matter can only, at best, provide a small fraction of the reading requirements of the ordinary citizen. While the religious literature societies do in fact publish a fair amount of material for children and adults on general topics, their resources are barely equal to meeting their strictly religious commitments and cannot be relied upon to provide non-religious literature in the variety and quantities required. I shall return later to some consideration of the recent activities of the Christian bodies in the field of literature. The point which I wish to make here is that, in spite of the far from negligible efforts which they have been and are making, the scale of the problem is such that only government money, whether provided nationally or internationally, can make possible any significant contribution to its solution.

Experience in many countries has now established the principle that the most economical and efficient machinery for dealing with the problem is the setting up of a specialised organisation—usually known as a literature bureau—equipped and staffed both to meet particular needs at a particular time and to promote the growth of conditions in which, when the literacy campaign shall have achieved its objectives, a self-supporting literature 'industry' can flourish. Most of the literature bureaux so far established have been subsidised by government, though they customarily enjoy some degree of autonomy and co-operate freely with religious and voluntary bodies at work in the field.

I am fortunate in being able to provide, in an appendix to this book, a detailed account by Wilfrid F. Jeffries of the history, organisation and work of the North Regional Literature Agency which he founded in Nigeria and directed from 1954 to 1956. This is of great interest as a first-hand description of the practical work involved in such an undertaking and of the way in which it was tackled in the particular circumstances of Northern Nigeria at the relevant time. In other circumstances and at different times, other methods and techniques may be appropriate. A considerable amount of information and advice is contained in two UNESCO publications: *The Provision of Popular Reading Materials* (Monographs on Fundamental Education, No. XII), published in 1959; and *Simple Reading Material for Adults: its Preparation and Use* (Manuals on Adult and Youth Education, No. 3), published in 1963. Both these important volumes were compiled under the general editorship of Charles G. Richards, who was for several years Director of the East African Literature Bureau, but they include the testimonies and comments of experts from many areas. Since Africa tends to attract a good proportion of attention in this context, the earlier volume is perhaps of particular interest, in that the detailed studies included in it are drawn mainly from Asia and Latin America.

The functions of a literature bureau (using this as a convenient term to cover organisations which may take several forms, including government departments, public corporations or subsidised unofficial agencies) may be considered as divided into two parts, though the borderline between them is not very definite. One is to produce literature directly required by the government for putting its policies into practical effect. Such literature will include school textbooks, primers for literacy campaigns, transitional reading material for neo-literates, posters, leaflets, etc., about hygiene, agriculture, government regulations and the like. This kind of literature is generally produced to order as required by the government departments or agencies concerned, and the cost is chargeable to the ordering authorities. The second function is to publish on its own account reading material for those who can read, but for whom sufficient literature suitable to their needs and reading ability is not available and is unlikely to become available through the ordinary operations of commercial publishing. Such reading material may cover a wide field of publication: books and booklets, magazines, newspapers, practical manuals, recreational matter, original work and the translation or adaptation of work written in other languages. The cost of these publishing operations is a direct charge on the budget of the bureau, though to some extent it should be offset by revenue from sales.

The size and scope of the literature bureau, the extent to which it performs these functions, and the staff which it needs to employ, will vary according to local circumstances and resources. It will, however, generally require as a minimum a director qualified in publishing experience and business methods and knowledge of at least one of the local languages; an expert in book production to be responsible for the editorial and production work on projects that have been approved; a staff artist; a writer who can advise and train local authors; a secretary, a registry clerk and an accountant with the necessary ancillary clerical staff. Since literature bureaux are a comparatively recent invention, there is not as yet a large pool of experienced personnel on which to draw for securing such staffs; but a fair number of people have now been long enough on the job in different parts of the world for something like a professional approach to the problem to be discernible. Amongst those who have made important contributions to the accumulation of knowledge on the subject are Charles Richards, whom I have already mentioned; Dr Rupert East, who directed the Gaskiya Corporation in Nigeria and also worked in Pakistan and Venezuela; G. H. Wilson who pioneered this work in Central Africa; Bruce Roberts, who also worked in that area and in the South Pacific; Mushtaq Ahmed, of India; and Dr Seth Spaulding of the Office of Education, Washington.

The balance of activity between the two functions of the literature bureau will naturally differ from country to country. In India, for example, a very large number of agencies produce a 'vast amount' of reading matter, especially in Hindi, for people who have reached the stage of functional literacy; but there is a serious dearth of material to bridge the gap between that stage and the requirements of basic literacy. Yet, as Mushtaq Ahmed has pointed out, this is the vital period for developing reading skills and a desire for further learning.[3] In India, therefore, it seems probable that any national or state agencies constituted to deal with the problem will concentrate upon the development of what are there termed 'first-stage supplementary books'.

The Latin-American Fundamental Education Press, sponsored jointly by the Organisation of American States and UNESCO, has, as its name implies, an objective that is limited to beginners in reading. It produces specially written booklets composed in very simple terms and using a vocabulary of familiar words, covering the basic knowledge and skills taught in the elementary schools: arts, mathematics, social and natural sciences, civics, health, economic and social affairs, agriculture and labour, and leisure reading. A Fundamental Education Library has been planned, consisting of 100 basic booklets on the above subjects, designed 'to be an encyclopaedia of information for everyday living'. In 1953–55 forty booklets were issued with a total printing of $2\frac{3}{4}$ million copies.[4]

In India and Latin America, there exist comprehensive literatures for the fully literate reader, and demand is catered for by normal publishing organisations. The Burma Translation Society was founded in 1947 to deal with a situation in which virtually no literature, apart from some religious and political publications, existed in the language of the country. Officially the society is a private body, but it was sponsored by the prime minister, U Nu, and other government leaders and is largely financed by government funds, both in the form of grants and privileges and because the government is the principal customer for its publications. As its name implies, the Burma Translation Society was founded with the object of providing the Burmese people with a literature in their own language which would put them into touch with world affairs, modern developments in science and technology, and the accumulated knowledge and wisdom of the ages. After some years successfully spent in this work, the society began to change its emphasis, realising that the most immediate need was to give the rural communities, which constitute the bulk of the population, simple reading matter to communicate ideas and information enabling them to improve their way of life.

Fortunately, Burma has no language problem since, though there are some local dialects, over 90 per cent of the people speak Burmese. For the benefit of the neo-literates who were emerging in growing numbers as a result of government mass education activities, a series of 'People's Handbooks' was prepared. A second series, at a rather more advanced level, was 'beamed' at the people who had graduated to the next stage of proficiency in reading. Both series covered a range of six subjects: agriculture, health, practical economics, civics, general culture, and recreation. Another venture of this society has been a popular illustrated magazine which has appeared monthly since 1951. It is mainly purchased by government and distributed free to schools and reading rooms, to the average extent of one copy to each of the 18,000 villages in the country. The contents of the magazine include news, practical instruction and the inculcation of civic ideals. The treatment, as in the handbook series, is largely in story form.

The countries of Africa provide further variations on the theme. Most of them suffer from widespread illiteracy and a multitude of mother tongues in which little or no literature of any sort existed before recent years. On the other hand, for historical reasons, the common language of educated people in most of them is that of the colonial power by which until lately they were ruled, or still are ruled—English, French or Portuguese—and this educated section of the community (a minority but a growing one) has access to all the literature available to people of similar education in Europe. At this level, the work of a literature bureau may lie mainly in improving distribution and encouraging the work of local authors, until such time as normal commercial publishing and bookselling and the customary library services of a civilised country have been sufficiently developed to take care of themselves. For the most part, therefore, in Africa, the activities of a bureau will be concerned with literature in the vernaculars; and this will include, according to local circumstances, both mother-tongue literature in a variety of languages of restricted local use, and literature in languages, such as Arabic, Swahili or Hausa, which are widely used as a second language or *lingua franca* by people for whom they are not the mother tongues.

Most of the African governments now have, under various names and various terms of reference, officially sponsored and subsidised organisations charged with the duty of producing, publishing and distributing literature at various levels in the vernaculars. Such, for example, is the Bureau of Ghana Languages, originally called the Gold Coast Vernacular Literature Bureau, which since 1951 has been producing booklets, translations, miscellaneous literature and newspapers in the predominant languages of the country. Where small pockets exist of languages spoken by an insufficient number of persons to support any considerable body of literature, the people concerned have been encouraged to become literate in one of the more generally used languages of the country.[5]

In some cases governments have combined effectively to create organisations covering a wide area, thus enabling experience to be pooled and overhead expenses kept to a minimum. Such organisations are the South Pacific Literature Bureau, maintained by the international South Pacific Commission; the East African Literature Bureau, established with headquarters at Nairobi, Kenya, and branch offices in Tanganyika (Tanzania) and Uganda; and the Northern Rhodesia and Nyasaland (Zambia and Malawi) Joint Publications Bureau established with headquarters at Lusaka, Zambia. Both these latter organisations have developed into large publishing bodies with a considerable output of literature in wide variety. Geographically, the work was broken down to the requirements of different areas by the establishment of regional committees. Financially, the publications side was provided at the outset with a 'float' (£25,000 in the case of the East African Bureau and £5,000 in the case of the Northern Rhodesia and Nyasaland Bureau). During the first fourteen years of its work the East African Bureau spent some £200,000 in publishing and the fund in 1962 stood at £25,000 in cash and £30,000 in stock.

Enough has been said to show that, as a result of the experience of all these pioneer efforts in different parts of the world, a body of authoritative guidance is now available concerning the organisation and procedures of literature bureaux and also as to the form and content (allowing for local variations of need and custom) of the publications which the bureaux may be called upon to sponsor. The UNESCO monograph on *The Provision of Popular Reading Material* contains, as well as the case-histories to which I referred earlier, an important section which deals in some detail with the questions that arise in organising and administering a bureau. The same ground is covered, though in summary and in less detail, in the concluding chapter of the manual on *Simple Reading Material for Adults: its Preparation and Use* to which I have also already referred. The main purpose of this manual, however, is to provide practical guidance on the actual production of the literature specially required for the transitional stage between neo-literacy and full literacy. The chapters deal with every stage from the first assessment of the general requirements to the particular problems of subject-choosing, writing, vocabulary and style, language and translation and adaptation, illustrations in line, colour and half-tone, testing of texts, editing, copy preparation, layout, typography and proof-reading.

A number of principles which apply generally, irrespective of variations in local circumstances, may now be said to have been established by experience. Books for readers at this level must be short. 'The more you try to say, the less is remembered.' About forty pages seems to be the desirable maximum. Some subjects will need more, in which case breaking up into two volumes should be considered; some will need much less.

Sentences too should be short, say a dozen words, and confined to making one point. Direct address to the reader is preferable to impersonal or abstract statement. Active verbs should be used rather than passive.

Illustrations, though adding to the cost of production, are usually necessary for the success of the book, but they must be planned and tested as rigorously as the text. Colour helps, but must be used intelligently.

The story form is often the best method of communicating the idea of the book, but it should not be overdone. 'When an adult is interested in a subject, he will generally appreciate a straightforward presentation of the material.'[6]

One of the first things that a new literate will want to read is a newspaper. Several literature bureaux set out to satisfy this need. 'In Israel there is a special newspaper which has sections of varying difficulty, enabling the new literate, as he progresses, to read an ever larger amount of the same paper, to which he is encouraged to remain loyal as he improves in reading skill.'[7]

Newspaper production is a technical business and expensive, unless a large enough circulation can be guaranteed to cover production costs through sales and advertisement revenue—a condition unlikely to be satisfied in the context of reading matter for new literates. Much interest, therefore, attaches to a project for producing rural newspapers by mimeograph (that is to say, typewritten and reproduced by stencil) which has been worked out in Liberia. The case history of this project, with detailed guidance, based on experience, for those who might wish to adopt the plan elsewhere, is recorded in the UNESCO publication, *Reports and Papers on Mass Communication*, published in 1965. Written by Robert de T. Lawrence, an American journalist who was adviser to the Liberian Information Service in 1963, this essay describes how the scheme was planned with a view to producing five newspapers in the first instance. In fact, as many as thirty were eventually published, in response to an overwhelming demand from the village people. Editors were trained, encouragement and advice were given, but there was no question of subsidising the publications. They were intended to be self-supporting—and they were. The author claims that any country, using its existing resources, 'could match or even exceed the accomplishment of Liberia, and do it in the course of one year. The speed with which this can be accomplished is dependent only on how soon the small amount of effort is expended to set the ball rolling.'[8] Certainly a convincing case is made out, and the detailed directions both to organisers and to the editors on the job are extremely practical and encourage optimism as to the future of this very useful type of publication.

So far I have been considering literature which is provided either by government or by philanthropic bodies in the interests of the new literate. It would be impossible to make a full catalogue here, but passing reference at least should be made to the specialised courses in 'literacy journalism' and writing techniques initiated by Dr Frank Laubach and conducted by his son, Dr Robert S. Laubach, at Syracuse University and other institutions in the United States.

Such instances as are known to me of attempts by commercial publishers to meet the need for reading matter at this elementary level of literacy have not, so far, been encouraging. For example, in the 1950s, an enterprising London publishing house, (Buffalo Books, Ltd.), wishing both to help development in Africa and to establish a business there, devised a scheme for producing an illustrated periodical, to be entitled *Forward*, for the special benefit of the new reading public on the west coast. African artists were engaged, and local authorities were consulted about the contents, which were designed as a judicious combination of instruction and entertainment. The cost of producing this periodical in colour could be covered only by printing very large editions, and this was to be achieved by reproducing the coloured and black and white illustrations in bulk, and overprinting them with the letterpress in various vernacular languages. Even so, it was found that an economic selling price could not be less than ninepence a copy. Direct sales to the public could not be expected to be large at this figure, and the success of the venture depended on the willingness and ability of the government literature agencies to purchase quantities for redistribution. The Gold Coast Vernacular Literature Bureau agreed to give the project a trial and to take up copies of the pilot issue. The result appears to have been very satisfactory, so far as concerned the reception of the periodical by the public. The Bureau, however, found the cost too high for it to be able to guarantee a regular bulk order, and the project eventually had to be abandoned.

There remains for consideration a class of reading matter which is published in the interests of the producer, with the object of persuading the reader to accept a particular ideology, to support a particular party or political programme, or to spend his money on certain goods: in other words, propaganda and advertisement. 'Literacy is the Road to Communism' was the Russian slogan, and so, of course, it is: a fact which might make the anti-communist suspicious of literacy until he should reflect that it is also the road to everything else. For the missionary, it is the road to Christianity; for the humanist it is the road to a better social order; for the economist it is the road to profitable development of the human and material resources of the community. Literacy, in short, is neutral: what matters with it, as with every other tool, is how it is used.

At the same time, there is no escaping the fact that every kind of reading matter from the most elementary stage upwards, inevitably possesses a slant of some kind. The simplest statement involves certain assumptions about the meaning and purpose of human life and the universe around us. Indoctrination can begin at a very early stage of literacy. The distinction between information and propaganda is not easy to draw.*

Large quantities of political propaganda do in fact pour into the developing countries from many quarters, and some of it

* 'Orthodoxy, my Lord', said Bishop Warburton in a whisper, 'orthodoxy is my doxy, heterodoxy is another man's doxy.'

finds its way to the new readers. On the whole, however, it tends to be produced in international or widely used languages rather than in the local vernaculars and to use a vocabulary and style beyond the scope of the neo-literates who are being considered in this chapter. It will therefore be more usefully discussed in the pages which follow. Meanwhile, it is fair to note that reading matter for new literates can be and generally is used to give them a balanced outlook which will help them to judge on their merits whatever propositions may be put to them by interested parties.

11

MATERIAL FOR MATURE READERS

COUNTRIES VARY very greatly in the facilities which they offer to people who have learned to read and wish to use their gift of reading to gain knowledge or entertainment. Much depends on whether there already exists, in the language which they can read, an established literature, in which case it is only a question of their adding themselves to the circle of readers. This is, of course, the position in countries where an international language is the language in which mass literacy is taught. The people of such countries will want material suitable to their reading ability and relevant to their way of life, and this may present a problem. The resources of the whole literature available in the language concerned are, however, there to be drawn upon, and the problem is nothing like so difficult as that of countries where the language of literacy is one with no literature or with a literature of very limited scope.

Although India, as has already been noted, has a great shortage of elementary literature for the earlier stages of literacy, it is very much better off in more advanced material, especially in the Hindi language. This material is produced not only by government agencies but by a number of voluntary societies and missionary bodies and also by commercial publishers. Both in India and Pakistan there is no dearth of established literature, particularly in the fields of religion and history, or of writers capable of adapting or abridging the classics for the benefit of new literates. There is, however, need for development of the pro-

134

duction of practical handbooks and instructional material which will help people to improve their standards of living. This is also the case in Ceylon—a comparatively literate country—where much of the available popular reading material consists of traditional and topical ballad verse which circulates in large quantities and is much appreciated for recreational reading.[1]

By contrast with these Asian countries, most of the countries of tropical Africa possess little or no ready-made literature for the new reader. Only those people who can read English or French and have access to books in those languages can get very far beyond the elementary stage. Much thought and effort is therefore being directed towards broadening the range of vernacular literature and improving the supply and accessibility of literature in European languages which has a special value or appeal from the viewpoint of the African reader. The problem is a complex one, and its many aspects call for several varieties of treatment which will be discussed later in this chapter.

Latin America, again, differs from the other major areas of illiteracy in certain important respects. In all countries of the area the Spanish or Portuguese language is the official and national tongue and there is no need or demand for creating a sophisticated literature in the vernacular languages spoken by the indigenous population. There are also highly developed publishing organisations in Mexico, Argentina and Brazil as well as in several of the other countries. The principal difficulty lies in the general poverty of the mass of the people, who cannot afford to buy books at commercial prices. It is therefore through financial assistance to publishing bodies, libraries and distributing organisations that a wider circulation of literature can most effectively be encouraged.

One of the first things a man wants to read when he is able to do so is a newspaper. The extent to which newspaper services are available varies very greatly from one country to another, and from area to area within the same country. To operate with any degree of efficiency and to be able to sell the paper at a price at which people will buy it (which necessitates a substantial revenue from advertisements) a newspaper publisher must be assured of a large circulation and regular and quick distribution. Obviously these conditions are more easily satisfied in towns or areas which are densely populated and have good internal communications than in rural districts where people are scattered in small and isolated settlements. According to UNESCO, while the number of copies of daily newspapers averages ten to every 100 persons for the whole world, 'the level falls as low as eight copies in South America, four in Asia and just over one in Africa'.[2] These averages are, however, in themselves misleading, since in South America, for example, Argentina, Chile and Uruguay have a highly developed daily press, whereas in some of the other countries the number of copies per 100 persons may be no more than five or even less. The average for Asia takes account of the very high circulation figures of Israel, Japan, Hong Kong and Singapore. In most of the Asian countries the actual figures range downwards from three to less than one per 100 persons: and circulation is confined mainly to the large towns. The general position is not, in fact, very greatly in advance of that in Africa.

Those who may wish to go into details of the daily press will find them clearly set forth in the UNESCO booklet, *World Press*, published in 1964. In the present context the daily newspapers are less relevant than the papers and periodicals, mostly non-daily, which are specially produced for the benefit of the populations now beginning to emerge from the state of general illiteracy.

As is not surprising, perhaps the most highly organised country in this respect is the Soviet Union, which possesses nearly 6,700 newspapers of all types ranging from the national dailies published in Moscow and reproduced in other large cities to roneotyped bulletins issued to the workers in factories and collective or state farms. In addition there are over 4,000 periodicals and magazines. A large proportion of these newspapers and other publications appear in local Soviet languages, and some also in foreign languages. The Soviet Union, however, is a country which has solved for itself the problems of illiteracy. Mainland China is less advanced in this respect but here also the news service is highly organised. A vocabulary of about 1,000 characters has been devised, and a nation-wide network of publication and distribution has been established, so that the policies and views expressed in the main national dailies filter down from the capital and large cities to the rural areas and factories. In every city street and village someone is officially employed to maintain a 'wall newspaper' on paper or blackboard and to read it aloud to illiterate persons.

India may be said to stand at the opposite extreme. There the well-established press tradition is based on private enterprise and largely on the use of the English language. Since the country gained independence there has been a marked increase in the number of papers and periodicals published in Hindi and other Indian languages. 'The Indian Government's Press Registrar shows that as many as 1,000 newspapers—usually in the Indian languages—are started each year. But most of these are amateur ventures which fail soon after their foundation.'[3]

Africa can show several examples of newspaper and periodical publication definitely designed for the new literates. In Ghana, apart from the English dailies and other English or vernacular publications produced by private enterprise, religious bodies or public corporations, there are several fortnightly or monthly papers published by the Bureau of Ghana Languages in eight languages of the country. Nigeria has a more developed press with more general national distribution than most other African countries. Here also there is an exceptionally high degree of African private enterprise in the press field. There are several African publishing organisations which produce papers in a variety of local languages. Reference is made in the Appendix to the origins of the semi-official Gaskiya Corporation, which continues to issue vernacular periodicals. In general, the Nigerians who have learned to read need not lack reading matter. As elsewhere, the problems are largely those of finance and distribution. On the eastern side of Africa, the East Africa Literature Bureau at Nairobi produces a periodical specially designed for adult literacy classes, magazines in English, Swahili and Luganda and a magazine for school-children. The periodical *New Day* published in Uganda is a notable contribution by the Christian Church to the need for informative popular reading matter in that part of the world.

Newspapers and periodicals have their essential part to play, but in the end it is the book on which people must rely for true and lasting satisfaction. 'Books', says Dan Lacy, Managing Director of the American Book Publishers Council, Inc., 'are an indispensable instrument in all the processes of a developed society. . . . No advanced economy or society can function and no less developed society can advance, without making a major, intensive use of books. . . . One of the principal problems of any development program is, hence, to assure the availability of the books, and the means for producing and using them, that will be required.'[4] This is perfectly true as a general statement, but it is obvious that the need is not just for books but for the right kind of books: and what is the right kind? In the essay from which I have just quoted, Dan Lacy goes on to observe that books have two different roles in promoting natural development. One is to convey information from developed countries to the developing country. This means taking books as they stand and placing them in libraries and other institutions where there are librarians and students who can keep and use them.

The other role is that of disseminating information within the developing country. This is a much more difficult matter, for existing books as they stand are hardly ever suitable for the purpose, even if it were practically possible for them to be imported in the numbers required. The books needed for general reading and dissemination of knowledge in any country must be specially written and produced in relation to the cultural, social and economic circumstances of the country. Preferably they should be produced within the country and written by indigenous authors. This calls for a planned effort to provide the conditions necessary for successful publishing: not only the discovery and training of authors and editors but the assurance of adequate supplies of paper, printing presses, distribution machinery, library services and working capital. It calls also for the establishment of organised arrangements for ensuring that the books produced will in fact be used in educational institutions and by the public. The effort cannot therefore be considered as a self-contained exercise: it must be seen as an integral factor in the general development plan of the country and must have the necessary priorities and resources allocated to it. A development plan which fails to take account of this, as well as of the need for basic literacy teaching, will lose much of its effectiveness and value.

The creation of *literature* is not a thing which other people can do for a nation: the nation must do it for itself, for no external authority, however well-intentioned, can do more than help. Yet help is a necessity for most of these countries, if they are to break out of the vicious circle. In recent years much serious consideration has been given to the question of the help that can be most effectively given by the developed countries and will be most readily accepted by the countries which are developing.

The sources of help are: international organisations, in particular UNESCO; individual governments willing to devote some part of their public funds to overseas aid; voluntary bodies and societies, especially those initiated by Christian missionary endeavour; and private organisations such as Franklin Book Programs Inc. of New York. Commercial publishers cannot be expected to assist unless some profit is to be had. In many of the developing countries the provision of school textbooks is a profitable business and attracts enterprising publishers; but much has to be done before the adult public can offer a market on any large scale, and the efforts of publishers in this field must inevitably be limited in the meantime.

The forms which help may take are: money; technical assistance and advice; gifts in kind, that is to say books and equipment. Money is the simplest sort of help, but not easy to come by. The funds available either to international organisations or to national governments for aid to the developing countries are limited, and there are far more calls upon them than can possibly be satisfied. Literature has to take its place in the queue, and there are so many pressing and more immediately obvious claimants that the place is unlikely to be a high one, whether the matter is looked at from the point of view of the donor or from that of the receiver. The voluntary sources of assistance are in a little better case, but not much. The societies and organisations which exist specifically for the promotion of communication through the printed word will naturally be ready and eager to use their funds in direct aid of literature projects. But the funds, though substantial and increasing, are exiguous in relation to the size of the problem. These bodies must unavoidably be selective in offering financial assistance, and grants will usually be in the nature of 'pump-priming'. The main sources of voluntary financial help are the Christian organisations, and their primary concern is to promote the Christian faith. It is, however, increasingly recognised in Christian circles that the term 'Christian literature' is not to be narrowly interpreted as confined to Bibles, prayer and hymn books, theological works and religious tracts, but should be considered as embracing all literature which helps the reader to lead a full life and to build up a peaceful and well-ordered society based on recognition of the rights and responsibilities of the individual.

This growing conviction found expression in 1962 at a 'Consultation' arranged at Bethel-bei-Bielefeld in West Germany by the Division of World Mission and Evangelism of the World Council of Churches. The result of this was the establishment by the World Council of a Christian Literature Fund, consisting of not less than $2 million dollars of new money to be raised over a five-year period from the donor countries and used to supplement the work of existing agencies. The administration of the Fund has been placed under the direction of Charles Richards, to whose notable contribution to the problem of producing reading matter for the peoples of the developing countries I have already referred.

In the United States, the main religious organisation for promoting these services is the Committee on World Literacy and Christian Literature (familiarly known as Lit-Lit), which was founded in 1943 and took into its scope the work previously done by a committee of the American mission boards and the campaigns initiated under their auspices by Dr Frank Laubach. It is financed by money provided by these boards and from other sources, and uses its funds to subsidise literacy projects (mainly in the vernacular languages), personnel training and improvement of distribution, according to the needs and requests of the local literature committees of the Christian Councils in the countries concerned.

Canada, West Germany, Holland, Sweden, Switzerland and other countries contain religious organisations which in varying degrees support literature work overseas. Apart from the United States, however, the principal source of assistance is Britain. Here, under the general leadership of the Archbishop of York (Dr F. D. Coggan), a campaign entitled 'Feed the Minds' was launched in 1964, with the dual object of increasing the annual revenues of the British and Foreign Bible Society and the National Bible Society of Scotland, and of raising a fund of £1 million for Christian literature. This fund, known as the Archbishop of York's Fund, was to be used to provide the British share of the World Council of Churches' Christian Literature Fund, and otherwise to assist such projects in the field of literature as the Trustees might select. The existing agencies which jointly sponsored the campaign were the two Bible societies, the Society for Promoting Christian Knowledge, and the United

Society for Christian Literature, and it was to be expected that these bodies would form the main channels through which assistance from the Fund would be made available.

If the opportunities for direct financial aid are restricted, there is ample scope for technical assistance and advice, and help of this kind is forthcoming in good measure from many quarters. In the forefront is UNESCO, which has promoted and is conducting so many activities in this field that it would be impossible to catalogue them all here. Some examples must suffice.

One of the most important services offered by UNESCO is the organisation of research and collection of information which is made available to governments and field workers through a variety of publications. Several of them have already been mentioned and have been heavily drawn upon in the compilation of this book. More will be found listed in the Reading List. Another important service is the arrangement of conferences, seminars and other meetings at which ideas are exchanged and experience pooled, and the publication for general information of the proceedings, conclusions and significant documents.

Generally, the headquarters of UNESCO in Paris form a focal point and centre for advice and guidance to all member states. In addition, local centres, dealing with specific needs in specific areas, are established where this is appropriate and practicable. For example, the UNESCO Regional Centre at Karachi administers, amongst other things, the South Asia Reading Materials Project. This was started in 1956 and originally covered Burma, Ceylon, India and Pakistan. Later, Iran, Afghanistan, Nepal and Thailand were added to the project area. At the outset, emphasis was laid on the production of reading matter for new literates, but as the work developed the programme was extended to deal with research, study and training in all aspects of book production, publishing and selling, and the provision and expansion of library services. Activities have included assistance for the publication of some hundreds of books for general read-

ers, the compilation of national bibliographies and the establishment of book promotion agencies.

The provision of books for the use of the peoples of the developing countries has been accepted as an important aim of the
United States Agency for International Development (AID).
Assistance from this quarter has been confined mainly to books
of an educational or technical character. The assistance is given
in a variety of ways, including the supply of copies of existing
American-published books, stocking of libraries with works of
reference, production and distribution of translated or specially
written books, training of book-industry personnel and financial
help by way of loan or guarantee to publishers or printers desiring to invest in the industry in the less-developed countries,
Special attention is given to the need for providing textbooks for
schools and educational institutions. Projects have been sponsored or helped by AID in many countries, including Latin
America, the Philippines, Vietnam, Indonesia, Thailand, Iran,
Nigeria and Nepal.

The United States Information Agency (USIA) also has an extensive programme of book supply. It does not itself publish
books, but through assistance to commercial publishers it pro-
motes the translation into local languages and the distribution
abroad of books 'which illustrate important aspects of American
life and culture or which contribute significantly to the exposure
of communist theory and practice'.

In the selection of titles about the United States or from the
field of American literature, the Agency looks particularly for
books which illustrate the leading role of the United States in
the pursuit of peace, which contribute to an image of the
United States as a strong and reliable partner to all other free
world nations, or which portray the American Society as typi-
fied by freedom of choice and its Government as characterised
by the rule of law rather than of men.[5]

As I said above, the line between information and propaganda is difficult to draw in a divided world. The Soviet and Chinese governments for their part spend a considerable amount of money and effort in promoting the sale and distribution in the developing countries of literature which proclaims the advantages of the communist way of life. Much of this literature—as indeed some of the literature emanating from the West—is polemic in character, aimed not only at extolling one point of view but at controverting the other side. Its inspiration is political rather than educational. Nevertheless, it includes much material which is not directly or overtly propagandist and is of positive value to the recipients. There is, for instance, a very large circulation in some countries of very cheap reprints of English classics, which in itself is a thing to be commended even if the intention is that the readers should be moved by gratitude to view sympathetically the source from which these benefits flow.

Like the American authorities, the British government has considered the provision of textbooks and educational material to have the first claim on the limited resources available for helping the developing countries in the field of literature. While up to 1960 the publication of educational books was largely left in the capable hands of the British commercial publishers active in this business, it has been recognised in recent years that some assistance from public funds is needed if the expensive books necessary for the use of students in institutions of higher education are to be made accessible at prices which the readers can afford. Arrangements have accordingly been made with certain publishers for the production of a series of subsidised books covering a range of scientific subjects and selected topics of general interest, to be sold at about one-third of the usual price. The scheme operates in India, Pakistan and a considerable number of other countries in Asia and Africa, and a total of well over 2 million books has been published in some 150 titles. The United Kingdom government, working through the British Council and other official and semi-official agencies, has also paid some attention to the training of journalists, writers, librarians and others concerned in the book industry. Technical assistance has been financed by funds made available under the Colonial Development and Welfare Acts and other provisions.

This kind of work has been strongly supported by the Christian bodies. These bodies no longer think in terms of exporting reading material to the 'mission field', except, of course, the Scriptures themselves. Their main object now is to help the local people to write and produce their own books. Effective help is increasingly being given through contributions of money and technical know-how to local organisations set up by the churches on the spot for the purpose. A notable example is to be found in the results of an 'All-Africa Christian Literature Conference' arranged by the African churches in 1961 at Kitwe in Northern Rhodesia (now Zambia). At this gathering it was agreed to establish two centres for literature work; one at Mindolo, Zambia, for English-speaking Africa, and one at Yaoundé, Cameroon, for French-speaking Africa. At these centres courses for writers and people involved in literature production are given and 'clearing-houses' maintained for the collection and dissemination of material to help the literature workers employed by the churches and Christian Councils in the different countries to carry out their tasks. These organisations are mainly financed from local sources, but they are assisted both financially and technically by the Western churches acting through the specialist agencies which I have already mentioned. The guiding principle was stated at the 1962 Bethel Consultation* by Dr Floyd Shacklock of the United States Committee on World Literacy and Christian Literature:

In Lit-Lit we say that even if it were possible to write and print a perfect Swahili book in our New York office, which of course we cannot do, it is not good enough to whip that book out to East Africa. Our work is not satisfactory until that book is planned, written, edited, published and sold in Africa, by the African Church.[6]

* See page 140.

On this principle the churches have been instrumental in setting up literary 'workshops' in many countries, and it is accepted that developments along these lines must claim a high priority in the programmes of the Christian bodies during the coming years.

I turn now to the question of gifts of books in kind, which are normally made to and through institutional or public libraries. The United States Information Agency and the Peace Corps operate schemes for presenting donated books to libraries, reading rooms and schools in developing countries. In the year 1963–64, nearly $1\frac{1}{2}$ million books were despatched to various parts of the world under these schemes. Three of the major American book clubs have given free subscriptions to about 1,000 foreign libraries.[7] A number of private American agencies, such as the African American Institute and the Freedom House Bookshelf, are also active in procuring books for despatch as free gifts to places and people in need of them.

Through the British Council, the United Kingdom has for many years sought to make a wide range of English literature accessible to the reading public overseas. Comprehensive libraries are maintained at the numerous British Council centres in Commonwealth and foreign countries. In India and Pakistan, these provide facilities for making expensive textbooks available to students and colleges on long-term loan. Though the British Council libraries are not intended as a substitute for public libraries, in some cases (as in Ghana) they have provided the basis on which a public library service has been created.

Some American efforts in the direction of arranging gifts of 'used' books appear not to have been entirely successful, and activities of this kind may clearly raise questions of some delicacy. In many of the developing areas, however, books are so scarce and the shortage of them so hampering to social and educational progress that little fear need be entertained of giving offence. In 1963, according to UNESCO, there were in the world '*hundreds of thousands* of schools which lack even such basic equipment as books and pencils, desks and blackboards'.[8] Many hundreds of thousands more possess little but the bare necessities of equipment, and certainly lack any supply of recreational reading material for the children. In most Commonwealth countries and some others, the young are taught English at an early stage and are taught *in* English during the latter part of their education. There is therefore an almost unlimited capacity to absorb English books for young readers which can be understood through the illustrations by children with only a limited knowledge of the language.

Such is certainly the experience of an unofficial British organisation which has a record of proved success in this field. It owes its inspiration to the Countess of Ranfurly who, when her husband was governor of the Bahamas in 1954, was shocked by the lack of books in the libraries of the out-island schools. She collected books privately for the schools, and later, finding that the case of the Bahamas was typical of many of the developing countries, she arranged with the English-Speaking Union to set up an organisation in London to deal with the problem on a Commonwealth basis, covering books for adults and older chilren as well as for infants. By 1966, nearly 2 million books had been sent out to fifty-nine countries; with the letters of appreciation pleas for more and more books kept flowing in. It was therefore decided to set up the Ranfurly Library Service as a non-profit-making company, and to seek to raise by public subscription the funds necessary to expand the output to $2\frac{1}{2}$ million books a year by 1969 and to carry the work to countries outside the Commonwealth in which English books are acceptable.

This service works on the principle that all books are given and all are delivered free of charge at their destination. The collection, sorting and packing is done by voluntary workers, and the shipping companies carry them at nominal or at no cost. They are received at the other end by directors of Education or other responsible people who have agreed to act as agents, and are distributed by them to schools, institutions, libraries, reading rooms, hospitals, police posts—wherever, in fact, they are most needed and will be best used. The only expenses incurred by the organisation are rent and the salaries of a small permanent staff. The cost of the operation is thus kept down to an average of less than sixpence per book delivered, the necessary funds being contributed by charitable trusts and private benefactors. Associated library services have been established in Australia, Canada and New Zealand, and also by the British organisation Voluntary Service Overseas.

In connection with fund-raising, it may be added here that UNESCO seeks to obtain money from the public in eighteen donor countries for the furtherance of its objects by means of a gift coupon scheme. Contributors are invited to choose projects from an approved list and to collect money to buy gift coupons which they then send directly to the authorities conducting the chosen project, who use them as a kind of international currency for buying scientific and educational equipment and supplies. The eligible list at present includes literacy projects in thirteen countries of Asia, Africa and Latin America.

I2

DISTRIBUTION

THE SOCIAL handicap, to overcome which is the aim of all that begins with literacy teaching, will be fully dealt with only when people can not only read but have the literature which they need, as and when and where they want it and at prices they are able and willing to pay. In free countries, a free press and free enterprise in publishing and selling literature are essential components in a sound and progressive society.

Publishing is a business. A demand for literature should create a supply, and it will, if the business is a paying one. So far as publishers are concerned, there need be no dearth of the reading matter which the public want if an economic market can be assured. In the countries which this book is mostly about, one of the main obstacles to establishing such a market is the high cost, coupled with the physical difficulty, of distribution. I have often been assured by publishers that, if the problem of distribution can only be solved, they will be ready and willing to do the rest.

The distribution of primers and class readers used in literacy instruction does not present a problem, for it is necessarily carried out as part of the literacy programme by the organising authority. As has been observed above, literature at this level is usually produced by government agencies, and scope for private enterprise is limited. Again, the distribution of school books is carried out or facilitated by the educational authorities, and commercial publishers find a ready and no doubt profitable market in this category of literature. Newspapers rarely attempt to cover a wide geographical area, but rely for their market on the population of the town or locality in which they are printed.

As with literacy itself, the Christian churches and religious societies have in many countries led the way in the selling and distribution of literature. Over the years, the Bible societies have established depots, distribution centres and shops in every area open to them and have organised local distribution by van, colporteur and any other available means to disseminate the Scriptures in the local languages as widely as possible. Their distribution work is, however, strictly confined to the circulation of the Scriptures and their facilities have not generally been at the disposal of those who have other literature, even if it be of a religious or educational character, to distribute. The Christian missions, which in so many places were the pioneers of education, have often been the founders of the local bookselling industry. In addition to Scriptures, they needed books, stationery and equipment for the church schools, textbooks for people being trained as catechists, teachers or pastors, hymn and prayer books for the congregations, and literature for members of the public who might want it. They very naturally set up their own organisations to procure and sell these goods, and in many cases a flourishing general trade was developed as educational progress created a more sophisticated class of customer. The pattern varied: sometimes the organisation was a local one owned and operated by a local church; sometimes it was the property of a home-based society which operated it in the interests of the local church and public.

In the early 1960s, I was privileged to be invited by the Christian Literature Council of the Conference of British Missionary Societies to make a survey of such information as could be obtained about the Christian bookshops throughout the world (with the exception of Europe, North America, Australia and New Zealand). The replies to the questionnaire which was sent out were given in confidence, but much of the information concerns matters of public knowledge. Various sources of reference were consulted, and a list of over 400 Christian bookshops was compiled. The total number is doubtless much greater; there are very large numbers of such shops, for example, in India, but much research would be needed to identify them all, especially as many are probably more in the nature of church bookstalls than what is generally understood as a bookshop. These, and those of the shops which are wholly or primarily concerned with the sale of Scriptures and religious literature are outside the scope of this book. Many of the shops, however, in various parts of the world which are run by religious bodies carry a considerable amount of general trade, and in several cases are the leading or indeed the only bookshops in their locality.

A notable example of religious enterprise in this field is the chain of bookshops established in Nigeria by the Church Missionary Society (CMS). These shops, set up in the principal centres where the society was at work, built up a flourishing educational business in connection with the church schools on which the country in the early stages of development largely relied for primary and secondary education. When it became no longer suitable for the society, as such, to own and operate them, they were transferred to a local company, the CMS Bookshops (Nigeria) Ltd in which the Anglican Church in Nigeria retained a controlling interest. There are at present some thirty-five of these shops in business. Other Christian bodies in Nigeria, notably the Sudan Inland Mission, which works mainly in the north, have also established bookshops doing a substantial general trade. The Church Missionary Society also established bookshops in Sierra Leone, and started shops in East Africa which were subsequently disposed of to the Educational Supply Association (East Africa) Ltd, and the Uganda Bookshops Ltd (a Church-controlled company). Another British body which has a notable record is the Society for Promoting Christian Knowledge (SPCK). This society has established four shops in what is now Tanzania and recently transferred their ownership to a local company representing the society. The SPCK has bookshops in South Africa and Rhodesia, and an important chain of shops in the Caribbean area. Those in Barbados, Jamaica and Trinidad are prominent in the local bookselling trade, and perhaps even more so are the shops in the smaller islands less well served by commercial booksellers. The associated Indian Society for Promoting Christian Knowledge is active in the subcontinent.

Yet another British society, the United Society for Christian Literature, has made a notable contribution to distribution especially in Africa. At Lusaka and Kitwe in Zambia the society maintains shops trading on a very considerable scale. Methodist, Presbyterian, Congregational and other British societies also have shops in various parts of the world: the Methodist shops in Ghana are a notable example. In Ghana also there is considerable bookselling activity by the Basel Mission of Switzerland, centred at Kumasi. The Danish Missionary Society is responsible for the bookshop at Aden.

The above is not intended as a complete summary of Christian bookselling activity in the developing countries, but only as an indication, by means of examples, of the important part which this activity has played and is playing in making general as well as religious publications accessible to the peoples of these countries, especially in regions where commercial bookselling would not as yet be an economic proposition. Indeed, the contribution of the religious bodies consists not only, or even chiefly, in the sale of literature over the counters. In the larger cities, such as Lagos, Accra, Kingston, Singapore or Salisbury, there are commercial bookshops available to the public and the religious shops have no monopoly or even any special attraction to the general customer except in so far as they may be able to offer better service than their competitors. Even when the religious shops have pioneered the business and set the pace, commercial enterprise is bound to show up as soon as a profitable trade is in prospect. In the early stages the established bookshops have some advantage over the new entrant to the business, since they can command better credit and more regular supplies than publishers may be willing to concede to operators of whom they have no experience; but this can only be a transient phase, and in many places successful bookselling businesses are being built up by enterprising local people. There is, however, little evidence as yet of large established bookselling concerns being involved to any great extent in the developing countries; presumably they are, very naturally, reluctant to open up business until there is a realistic prospect of its being profitable. From some knowledge of the affairs of some of the religious bookshops—and these by no means the least efficient or worst situated—I can say with confidence that no fortunes have yet been made by their sponsors.

The important thing, from the present point of view, is that these bookshops are not solely concerned with selling over the counter but are distributive centres covering areas where no bookshops exist. In order to supply the churches, mission stations and schools in their districts, they operate book vans and other media for transporting books and literature. Except in the case of the Bible societies' depots, which normally deal only in Scriptures, they send out by these means not merely religious literature but such general books as the public may need and be prepared to buy. They do this partly as a social service and partly because sales help to offset the costs and make the operation practicable.

For, in the conditions of the developing countries, it is the relatively enormous cost of distribution which most severely hampers the wide circulation of literature. At least one commercial concern which attempted to run (in West Africa) a mobile bookshop as an economic venture had to abandon the project as unprofitable. It is easy to talk of operating a book van, but one has to consider the hard facts. There is the capital cost of the vehicle and its equipment, the high cost of maintenance and running repairs, heavy depreciation. It has to be manned: a full-size van may need a crew of two. Even the small three-wheel 'scooter' type of vehicle which is coming into use for this service is expensive enough for all that it can be operated by one man, especially as a small vehicle can carry only a limited stock. Anyone so employed must be reliable, honest, a good driver and practical mechanic, knowledgeable about the books he is engaged to market, a good salesman, a linguist, capable of keeping accounts, prepared to undertake rough journeys involving prolonged absence from home. Such admirable Crichtons are hard to come by, and can command high salaries for less arduous kinds of employment. The limited capacity of the vehicle has to be filled mainly with low-priced goods carrying a very small margin of profit. It is obvious that an enormous number would have to be sold to cover expenses of the order involved, and it is not surprising that most of the book vans and mobile bookshops to be found in the developing territories are subsidised either by religious and charitable bodies or by the governments in connection with the operations of the literature bureaux.

At best, mechanised bulk transport can only take the goods to certain focal points from which any more widespread distribution to villages and hamlets will have to be organised. Here again, in areas where churches and mission stations are well spaced about the countryside, they provide a network of communications which can be and is used for the circulation of literature. Among many ingenious expedients which have been devised or improvised for dealing with the problem of distribution, mention here may be made of a scheme invented by the United Society for Christian Literature workers in Zambia. This consisted of engaging students who are going on vacation to take a supply of books with them to sell in their home neighbourhoods. They receive a commission on sales, and can indent for further supplies when they have exhausted the initial consignment. This is clearly a cheap and effective method of getting literature distributed in places which could only with difficulty be reached by other means.

A wide distribution of cheap and good literature is essential for social progress and no literacy campaign can be considered to have fulfilled its object and justified its expense unless the readers have before them the prospect of access to such literature. It is clear, however, that in many of the developing countries where the need is greatest, the problem of achieving this distribution is very far from being solved. It is, unavoidably, a question of money. Subsidies have to be produced from somewhere for the time being and for a long way ahead. The amount needed to do the job properly is far outside existing government or charitable resources.

In their replies to the questionnaire referred to above, a large proportion of the religious bookshops stated that the possibilities of expanding their business were very great—such adjectives as 'tremendous' and 'limitless' were used in some cases. The chief obstacles were lack of capital and of trained staff; there was also need of technical advice and guidance. One of the objects for which the Archbishop of York's Fund* was established was to help with finance in such circumstances, and some assistance has already been given. For example, the fund made a grant in 1966 to enable the Society for Promoting Christian Knowledge to open a new bookshop in Maseru, Lesotho (Basutoland). For the other two needs—trained staff and technical advice—help is available from various sources. The British literature societies assist in training booksellers both in their own countries and in the United Kingdom. In India, the Christian Literature Society does the same, and a number of successful 'Booksellers' Training Institutes' have been held. A useful handbook for booksellers has been prepared by the Reverend P. Penning of this society. On the technical side, one of the chief needs of the overseas bookseller is for guidance in the selection of books to import for stock from amongst the bewildering variety of publications issuing

* See page 141 above.

from the presses of the developed countries. Where government-sponsored literature bureaux exist, it is part of their function to assist distribution by advising booksellers of probable trends in demand and helping them by judicious selection to avoid landing themselves with a load of unsaleable stock. They can also help reliable people who are setting up as booksellers to make a start and obtain stock on credit terms from publishers, and they can encourage local enterprise by persuading schools and libraries to obtain supplies through them instead of ordering from abroad.

Help in the selection of books has for many years been a concern of the Christian bodies in Britain, Canada, the United States and elsewhere. Up to 1959, this concern—in relation to Africa—found expression in the work of an International Committee on Christian Literature for Africa which, among other activities, published a quarterly review entitled *Books for Africa*. After 1959, this committee ceased to exist and the work was gradually transferred to the Literature Clearing House for English-speaking Africa which was set up at Mindolo, Zambia, under the auspices of the All-Africa Churches Conference, with financial assistance from the American Committee on World Literacy and Christian Literature and from British and other missionary bodies.* This, however, is a general problem which affects many areas besides Africa and many communities with which the Christian churches are not in touch. There would, therefore, seem to be room for a periodical bulletin containing sufficient information about selected current publications of the paperback class in the English language to enable overseas booksellers to pick out those items which are best suited to the conditions of their own particular markets. A plan for producing such a periodical has been prepared, in fact, but the modest financial backing which would be necessary has not been obtainable.

So far we have been considering the distribution of literature

* See pages 141–2 above.

for sale to the public. In places where books are scarce and expensive, where the ordinary home contains little or no accommodation for keeping them, and climate and insects play havoc with them if they are not properly stored, libraries with borrowing facilities can be of great use. I am thinking here not of the public libraries which are fairly generally to be found in the large towns and cities, but of rural and village library services. This is a subject which has been given special attention in India. The system here varies from place to place, but it is the general rule that as far as possible every village where the people are literate or learning to become literate should have its library. The books are supplied by the state authorities and distributed through a system of communications which ends, perhaps, with a solitary cyclist making his way along the jungle path. The local school teacher or literacy instructor is put in charge and paid a small fee for doing this work. The costs are shared between the government and the local village authority. Many of the libraries have reading rooms attached, in which magazines and newspapers are provided.[1]

It would seem that, in this matter, India is somewhat ahead of most of the developing countries, though with help from various sources including UNESCO, the British Council, official and unofficial United States agencies, progress is being made in Africa and elsewhere. A special need is for assistance in training the village librarians to give more efficient service, since it is often found that, without positive encouragement to persevere and without guidance in the choice of books to read, the newly literate fail to take advantage of the facilities at their disposal. Moreover, the person who acts as village librarian is usually also the person who can best advise people on what books to buy for keeping and serve as agent for the sale of such books. He is the final link in the long chain of distribution.

Distribution, then, remains one of the most complex and intractable aspects of the problem of illiteracy. Yet, unless it can be dealt with adequately, the full benefit of literacy cannot be reaped. It follows that, in the planning of literacy programmes and the estimation of their costs in money and in manpower, provision should be included not only for the production of follow-up literature, which is now generally accepted as essential, but for practical measures to make literature available to the people everywhere at all levels within the range of their reading ability. Local circumstances differ, but it is a fair generalisation to say that this calls for a conscious and deliberate effort to bring together into an integrated system the different agencies—government, voluntary and commercial—which are concerned, and for frank recognition of the plain fact that distribution costs money which cannot in present conditions be recovered eventually from the customer. My impression, from study of such of the documents as have come my way, is that there is need for more research and authoritative guidance on this subject, and that distribution might well occupy a more prominent place in discussions and deliberations about illiteracy.

As Sir Francis Drake said in his famous prayer, when one is endeavouring any great matter 'it is not the beginning, but the continuing of the same, until it be thoroughly finished, which yieldeth the true glory'.

13

'A SOLEMN AND URGENT APPEAL'

As ONE turns the pages of the official reports and the news-letters of the organisations dedicated to the war against illiteracy, it is impossible not to be inspired by the excitement and achievement of so many efforts in so many parts of the world pressing towards the same end. To make a complete catalogue would fill many volumes. I can only here pick out a few illustrations at random.

For instance, in north-east Brazil, where the illiteracy rate is about 75 per cent, there is the *Cruzada ABC* which aims, with the support of the Presbyterian churches in America, to produce one million adult literates by 1970. There is, in Zambia, a similar target set by the Ministry for Community Development and Social Welfare. In Bolivia, there are 'nuclear schools', which have nothing to do with atomic physics but are rural schools used as the 'nuclei' of intensive drives against illiteracy. In Delhi, capital of India, with a quarter of a million illiterates, thousands are being taught to read in hundreds of classes organised by the city's Adult Education Board; and the same kind of thing is happening in other cities of India. In Iran, the army is on the march in this peaceful war. In Kenya and the Ivory Coast, television has been brought into the battle. In Cameroon, thousands of school teachers keep their schools open after hours, teaching the mothers the same lessons that their children have learned during the day.

Everywhere governments and municipal authorities, churches

and voluntary bodies, professionals and amateurs are engaged in the great work. Everywhere people are learning to read by the thousands a year. Again, to take some instances at random from the official statistics, the number of adults taught to read and write in 1962 was 191,273 in Ethiopia, 4,000 in Malawi, 18,783 in Rhodesia. In 1963 nearly 400,000 learned in Iran, 116,000 in Mexico.[1]

Reading the many reports, with their genuine record of success and their heartening evidence of so much good done to so many people, one is tempted, despite the immensity of the task, to take comfort from Clough's well-known lines:

> For while the tired waves, vainly breaking,
>   Seem here no painful inch to gain,
> Far back, through creeks and inlets making,
>   Comes silent, flooding in, the main.

One is tempted: but it will not do. While I have been writing this book, the number of people alive in the world has increased by something like the whole current population of the British Isles. In the six years 1961–66, the number of illiterates in the world has increased by something like 200 million. By how much (if at all) has the capacity of the world to feed its people increased in this period? The inability of 1,000 million people to read and write remains a millstone round the neck of progress.

This book was begun with the intention, which I trust has been faithfully carried out, of presenting an objective study of the world problem of illiteracy and not of pleading a cause. I hope, however, that any reader who has come so far with me may have become in the reading, as I have become in the writing, intellectually and emotionally seized by the magnitude and frightening urgency of this problem, and shocked at the sheer, stark, staring lunacy of a world which allows it to wait for a solution.

To wait how long, and for what solution? Up to now, men

have been comforted by the notion that, with the development of universal primary education, the problem will solve itself, not as quickly as the idealist might have hoped, but still within a generation or two. This, after all, is what has happened in the developed countries.

> Among the various cultural, social and economic factors related to illiteracy, obviously the most important is the education of children in primary schools. If all children of school age in any country attended school for a sufficient length of time, there would eventually be no adult illiterates in the population, except those mentally deficient and incapable of learning to read and write. It follows, therefore, that the best means of preventing illiteracy is to provide adequate education for all children.[2]

So stated an official UNESCO publication in 1957. And a Committee of the Commonwealth Education Conference of 1964 declared: 'The target for the main long-term effort to eradicate illiteracy is obviously in the schools.'[3]

The word 'obviously' is recurrent and significant. *Punch* used to have a feature called "Glimpses of the Obvious", in which it ridiculed portentous platitudes in public pronouncements. I have no wish to ridicule these statements, which are 'obviously' true, but the attitude they express is based on an illusion which has now been shattered. Quoting United Nations statistics, the *Population Profile* issued by the Population Reference Bureau Inc. of Washington, DC, on September 26, 1966, revealed that, of the 373 million school-age children in the world, only about 115 million—or 30 per cent—are in school; and of those who are, the majority will not even complete the primary course and will very likely relapse into illiteracy.[4] Even in a relatively advanced country such as Brazil, the average number of years of education completed is little over two and a half. In India (to quote the same authoritative source), there are 55 million children in school, of whom 40 million are in the elementary grades, and

132.5 million not receiving any formal education. The population of India is growing by at least 12 million a year. A parallel situation exists over vast areas of Asia, Africa and Latin America. Nearly 85 per cent of the births occurring in the world today take place in these 'developing' areas, and in many of these countries something like half the total population is under the age of twenty-one.

In the teeth of these stark and inescapable facts, only the most ostrich-like complacency could pretend that any substance remains in the conventional assumption that the problem of illiteracy will be solved in any foreseeable time by the operation of an expanded system of formal education. The countries concerned already devote a much greater proportion of their national budgets to education than do the developed countries—on an average some 15 to 20 per cent as against some 10 to 15 per cent. Even if there were no question of population increase, existing educational budgets would have to be doubled or trebled at once in order to provide primary schooling for anything like every child in the world. It is evident that this is simply not practicable. The difficulty is not merely financial. Schools have to be organised, built and staffed. Buildings might be improvised, but teachers cannot be produced by improvisation. They can only be obtained from the ranks of the relatively few people who, in the developing countries, have themselves had enough education to enter the teaching profession. Such people are naturally in great demand for other and usually less exacting and more remunerative or glamorous kinds of employment. Those who are willing to teach have to be trained; training institutions have to be arranged for, and this takes time—as does the training itself. Meanwhile, the number of babies born continues to increase, and the number of infants who die continues to decrease. To add the final touch of gloom, one must recall that, in any case, a large proportion of the children taught will get no lasting benefit from their schooling and will quickly reinforce the ranks of the adult illiterates.

It is a losing battle, and the conclusion cannot be escaped that the world will be lucky if it can keep the numbers of adult illiterates from continuing to increase above the thousand million during the rest of the century, however much it may succeed in reducing the percentages of illiterates in the population. Must the battle be lost? I believe not, if the strategy and tactics can be radically changed before it becomes too late. But it is a very big 'if'.

It took Russia from twenty to forty years to break the back of its problem of illiteracy. It took forty-four years to raise the literacy rate in the Philippines from something like 5 per cent to something like 75 per cent;[5] and at that rate it continues to stand. Since the number of adult illiterates remains fairly steady round about 4 million, the islands—after all the effort—still have to be classed as an 'area of illiteracy'.[6]

But the world has not now got forty or even twenty years to indulge in the luxury of illiteracy. The information I have examined in the writing of this book has led me to the firm conviction that there can be no half measures in tackling this problem. Nothing short of an all-out effort to achieve 100 per cent literacy (or as near as may be) *everywhere and at once* is worth doing. It is true that any literacy campaign does at least benefit some, perhaps many individuals, and that is all to the good. If, however, it succeeds only in making a proportion of the population literate, experience shows that at a certain level, varying from country to country, progress slows down or stops altogether, so that the percentage of illiterates in the country concerned remains stable or decreases very slowly. So long as that figure remains at, say, 25 per cent or more (and in several areas it is more like 75 per cent), the country is open to all the internal evils which result from 'two nations' of first-class and second-class citizens; while in its external relations it continues to be at a disadvantage compared with countries in which illiteracy has ceased to exist to any significant extent. The dangers of perpetuating these divisions in the present explosive world situation do not need to be demonstrated.

Of course, universal literacy cannot in itself make the world better, richer or more peaceful: that depends upon people. Literacy is a tool, and what matters is how people use it. But it does give people a chance which, without it, they do not have. It is arguable that people would have been happier if they had been left to pursue a simple way of life outside the turmoil of the contemporary world; but the argument is pointless, because the contemporary world is one world and all the people are involved in it together, whether they like it or not. We have to accept that fact, and make terms with the world as it is.

If it is agreed that an all-out effort must be made, the first and basic need is to get clear the relationship between literacy and 'education'. However right in principle it may be to regard the eradication of illiteracy as an educational problem, the practical fact is that, in this case, the best is the enemy of the good. Education involves much more than teaching people to read and write. That is the whole point. It is the 'much more' which the world cannot afford. Learning to read and write, whether by an adult or by a child, is not in itself education. It is the acquisition of a skill. It is in the same category as learning to walk, to talk, to prepare food, to sow seeds, hoe a field, ride a bicycle or swim. No one thinks of these things as education. They are skills which people need in order to live as human beings, and they are learned and taught within the circle of family or neighbourhood. Anyone who has learned them can teach others and does so as a matter of course, without any organised system.

It is surely evident that, if the politicians, planners and administrators would accept this view of the problem of illiteracy, an entirely new and simpler approach to its solution would at once become possible. By all means let educational programmes multiply and develop as fast as they can: no sensible person would wish to prejudice their progress. We are not here concerned, however, with those who can benefit from them. Our concern is with the millions of children who will never go to school and with the millions of adults who have never had the chance of going to school.

I yield to none in my respect for educationists and their work, but the fact that the problem of illiteracy has usually been considered as part of their department has tended to cloud the real issue. With the best intentions, the Teheran Conference of 1965 and other authoritative bodies have urged the importance of not treating the eradication of illiteracy as an end in itself and of integrating it with programmes of child and adult education. Nothing else was to be expected; yet I suggest that it is fundamentally wrong, in the practical situation in which the world is placed, to hold back the teaching of literacy while educational and social programmes are being developed. It is only by a complete reversal of traditional attitudes and by regarding the eradication of illiteracy not only as an end in itself, but as an end which must be attained at once and at all costs, that the world has any realistic hope of achieving it. Indeed, it offers the only hope of ultimately securing the necessary expansion of the educational system proper, and of ensuring that the money poured into it is not, as at present, largely wasted.

It is surely self-evident that a community in which everyone can read and write—whether or not it has a developed educational system—is in a far better condition to maintain itself and improve its position in the circumstances of the modern world than a community in which only a limited number of people are literate. Once people are able to read and write, they can educate themselves, provided that they have access to the necessary literature; this is an absolute condition of success. Not all will be able or willing to take advantage of the opportunities which literacy opens up to them, but many will. This is true of adults: it is even more true of the young. Moreover, the children who do go to school will not afterwards suffer the fate of those who return to an illiterate environment. Thus, the eradication of illiteracy will both make for greater general prosperity, enabling more to be spent on formal education, and also be a potent factor in progress towards the ideal of an educated society.

The target of concentrated effort must, therefore, be the establishment of a universal social custom by which all children, whether they go to school or not, will be taught to read and write as certainly and as naturally as they are taught to talk and walk. Whenever adults are taught literacy, they must at the same time have it impressed on them that their first duty is to pass the skill on to their own families and children. For a literate parent to have illiterate children should be stigmatised as a social disgrace. This will not, however, entirely solve the problem, since—as previous chapters have all too clearly shown—there are many communities in which there is no early prospect of even a majority of adults of the present generation becoming literate. In such cases, it will be necessary to extend the scope of literacy programmes to cover out-of-school children as well as adults.

But, if literacy is to be taken out of the purview of the education or 'community development' authorities, who is to look after it? If I were prime minister of a developing country, I would create a Ministry of Literacy and give the minister full cabinet rank and no other responsibilities. I doubt if it could be done any other way for, of course, it involves spending a lot more money than has hitherto been thought of as the suitable allocation for literacy work, and the money will have to be fought for at the highest level. In theory, it could be argued that the issue is so important that existing educational or other programmes should be cut back in its favour; but such a proposition would hardly be likely to receive general assent. It is more practical and more in the interests of the developing countries to assume that the cost of expanding literacy teaching for children and adults will need funds over and above existing budgets. What, then, would be involved?

The whole basis of the approach now suggested is that literacy instruction needs no special expertise or professional qualification. Anyone of average ability and intelligence can be trained to do it, and, once it ceases to be mixed up with other educational and social activities, it can be entrusted in the main to parents, relatives and public-spirited volunteers. Paid staff will be needed only for organisation and administration. Primers, teaching aids and reading matter at various levels will be essential, and this will be the chief item of expense; but for the most part it will only involve making larger printings of material already prepared in connection with school or adult education programmes.

It will be recollected that, in 1963, UNESCO estimated that it would cost about £700 million to make 330 million adults literate in ten years. If we double this to bring in the children, and add half as much again to the total to cover rising costs, a figure of £2,000 million (say, $5,600 million) may be taken to represent the rough overall cost of eradicating illiteracy. Though this is only a guess, I suggest that it may fairly be accepted as a reasonable estimate of the money required. £2,000 million is a huge sum, but it does not look so large if it is considered as £200 million a year for ten years. In the 1963 estimate, it was calculated that the developing countries themselves could produce 75 per cent—about £500 million— of the £700 million needed. One of the reasons why it was not practicable to proceed with the 1963 scheme was that those countries found it difficult to see their way to providing so high a proportion of the cost from their own resources. Nevertheless, it is fair to assume, for present purposes, that they should be able to find an average of £50 million a year, bringing the amount needed to be provided by the world collectively down to £150 million a year. The contribution towards this large sum which could be made by charitable sources might be quite substantial. Most fund-raising projects in this context have so far been initiated by religious bodies and mainly supported by members of churches. An appeal made on broad grounds of humanity and the public interest might well, if efficiently conducted, succeed in attracting a considerable response in the more affluent countries from people who are indifferent or even hostile to avowedly religious causes.

Even so, the bulk of the money would certainly have to come from government sources under international or bilateral aid schemes. It may be said that this is asking for the moon; it is precisely that. 'Whether we reach the moon is quite unimportant in comparison to the question whether we will help human beings to live, and to live as human beings are meant to live', says Dr Visser 't Hooft, former Secretary of the World Council of Churches.[7] I do not know, any more than any other member of the public, how much the world collectively is spending annually on space research and travel, let alone on producing weapons of destruction which would defeat their own object if ever used. One must guard against the dangers of oversimplification, of course, and it would be naïve to suppose that the great powers are at all likely to reduce their space and defence programmes in order to promote universal literacy, however sensible they would show themselves to be in doing so. Yet there is really no need to pose these as alternatives. In the scale of public expenditure by the affluent nations, the cost of eradicating illiteracy, if shared among them, would be trivial. If the world wants its people to be literate, it can have that and the moon as well. Moreover, it is an important consideration that, if the job is once thoroughly done, it will never have to be done again. The expenditure will not be recurrent.

It is beyond question that the establishment of universal illiteracy would enormously increase the human resources available for scientific and intellectual as well as economic progress. It would greatly improve the prospect of finding solutions to the problems arising from the growth in the world population. It might even affect that growth, for the undoubted statistical connection between population increase and low standard of living may also indicate a connection with a high rate of illiteracy. At any rate, it is a fact—coincidental or not—that, leaving out of account changes in population due to migration, the rise in numbers in countries with a low illiteracy rate tends to be appreciably slower than in those with a high illiteracy rate.

The Teheran Conference of 1965, 'convinced that the struggle against illiteracy, aimed at the total eradication from our planet of the scourge of ignorance, is a moral imperative for our generation', concluded its recommendations with:

A SOLEMN AND URGENT APPEAL

To the United Nations, its Specialized Agencies and, in the first place to UNESCO;

to regional bodies concerned with development in general and education in particular;

to non-governmental organizations which include assistance, direct or indirect, to education in their operational programmes;

to religious, social and cultural institutions;

to national and international foundations, both public and private

to educators, scientists and scholars, to economic and trade union leaders, and to all men of goodwill:

to do everything in their power to arouse public opinion with a view to intensifying and accelerating the world-wide attack on illiteracy; and in particular to exert their influence on all responsible leaders:

(a) to ensure that literacy work is an integral and essential part of every development plan in countries where illiteracy is rife;

(b) to increase, so far as may be practicable and appropriate, the national and international resources set aside for the fight against illiteracy;

(c) to make possible the provision of additional resources for development in general and for literacy work in particular as and when further funds become available through a reduction of military expenditures or for other reasons;

(d) to harness to the full all available information media for propagating the new concept of adult literacy;

(e) to ensure that priority in the allocation of available resources is accorded to the fight against the great human afflictions that constitute a major threat to peace, namely hunger, disease and ignorance, among which illiteracy occupies a place of key importance.[8]

'To arouse public opinion' . . . that is the root of the matter. This is supposed to be the age of democracy, the century of the common man. Yet—such is the fantastic paradox of the times—it is notorious that, in the great public matters which most nearly affect his life and welfare, the common man too often finds himself inexorably involved in programmes and policies for which he must labour, pay and die, but to which he is personally indifferent or positively opposed.

The will of the people cannot prevail unless it is founded on knowledge, clearly stated and effectively communicated. An illiterate people has neither access to knowledge nor ability to formulate its wishes and express them in the places where decisions are taken. If the common peoples of the world once realise what they are needlessly losing through the handicap of illiteracy, they will demand that, in the words of the Conference report, 'like all other forms of bondage, illiteracy—the enslaving of the mind—must be abolished'. If they once realise that, if only the authorities will take the trouble, it *can* be abolished, once and for all, within a reasonable time and at relatively moderate cost, they will demand immediate, resolute and effective action, and be ready to provide the necessary money and manpower.

If this book can in however humble a way help towards this essential mobilisation of public opinion it will have served its purpose.

APPENDIX

THE NORTH REGIONAL LITERATURE AGENCY, NORTHERN REGION OF NIGERIA
by
Wilfrid F. Jeffries
(*First Director, 1954–56*)

The North Regional Literature Agency was founded in 1954, by the government of the Northern Region of Nigeria. The mandate of the Agency was to provide vernacular reading material in support of the literacy campaign and in the general interests of public enlightenment during a period of intense development and social change. Material was needed but the reading public was not large enough to encourage commercial enterprise.

The Northern Region was a vast territory, sparsely inhabited by some 20 million people. Apart from a few largish towns where there was a cosmopolitan atmosphere and direct communication with the outside world, people lived in natural communities, pursuing agricultural and rural occupations, and there was a great variety of racial, linguistic and cultural differences. While there was a tendency towards a limited number of *linguae françae* for public business and a general desire to learn English, local languages and dialects were used for conversation and private affairs.

Politically the region was hurrying towards self-government of a democratic kind, and socially towards an important position in world economy as a producer of raw materials. An effect of the war was to accelerate the tempo of social development. The problem lay with the 'active' age-groups of people who had never been to school, and with all those who must enter those age-groups without schooling before expansion of school facilities could catch up with requirements.

At the end of the war, regionalisation was not clear cut, and the whole of Nigeria faced the problems of predominant illiteracy. Pilot literacy schemes in selected areas throughout the whole of the country were initiated to test methods of instruction and organisation and to break down prejudice. By 1949, the pilot schemes had proved their point and a separate North Regional Adult Education Office was opened, charged with the task of planning an intensive region-wide literacy campaign. During the next two years, devoted to the gradual spread of literacy schemes and to investigation and experiment, the magnitude of the task and its implications became clear. A comprehensive plan was drawn up in which other aspects of informal education parallel with, and complementary to, the literacy campaign were included; and, in 1952, an expanded Regional Adult Education Headquarters was set up.

Vernacular Literature and English Sections were created with an expatriate government administrative officer and an expatriate government education officer in charge respectively. The Vernacular Literature Section was responsible for the preparation of material in support of the literacy campaign and of general reading matter in the interests of public enlightenment, in the different languages required. The English Section was responsible for the study of method and the preparation of material for vernacular literates wishing to learn English, and to help people who already knew some English to improve their command of it by private study. Region-wide organisation for the literacy campaign provided not only the sources of essential information and the field for experiment, but also the lines of distribution for published material.

The development and expansion of the work of these production sections led, in 1954, to their separation from Adult Education Headquarters and establishment as the North Regional Literature Agency.

So that the picture may be complete and clear, mention must here be made of another institution already concerned with the development and production of vernacular literature in the Northern Region: the *Gaskiya* Corporation. This took its name from the officially sponsored weekly newspaper in the Hausa language which it published. The story of the Corporation is something of a parallel to that of the Literature Agency. Some forty or more years ago, a

Translation Bureau was opened as a section of the Education Department to make official translations and to prepare vernacular versions of readers and class books for primary schools—in Hausa mainly but a little work was done in one or two other vernaculars as well. In due course, the Translation Bureau became the Literature Bureau when work was put in hand on original productions. Attempts to interest the general public in reading for pleasure were not successful, but there was ample scope for work on school readers, and the craft of original writing in the vernacular was introduced. The work of the Bureau culminated in the issue of a Hausa newspaper with a Hausa editor. The full name chosen for the paper was *Gaskiya ta fi kwabo*, which meant that the truth it contained was more valuable than the penny charged for it. The books published by the Bureau were printed overseas but the newspaper was printed on a local press belonging to a missionary society.

The next development was the creation of a government-sponsored corporation, equipped to print newspapers and other publications, to edit and publish the Hausa newspaper, now commonly called *Gaskiya* (Truth), and a complementary English-language newspaper called *The Nigerian Citizen*; to provide translations; and to produce such vernacular literature as was required (which continued to be mainly for schools). At the same time, the *Gaskiya* Corporation was concerned with the establishment of a standard Hausa orthography, and with the controlled development of the language which, in a newspaper reporting events in a changing world, must find means of expressing new ideas. From its inception the literacy campaign was able to make use of the editorial experience and printing services that the *Gaskiya* Corporation could offer.

The scheme began at once. Primary school methods and class books were recognised as being unsuitable for work with adults, and the Hausa newspaper, *Gaskiya*, was necessarily designed as a national paper for people of some education with experience and general knowledge beyond the range of the peasant population for whom the literacy campaign was intended. A comprehensive primer for use in literacy classes was prepared and published, and work began on a programme for 'follow-up' reading matter, including a periodical. The pilot literacy schemes in the region were conducted in the Hausa language, with one exception. This exception was the use of the Tiv language for a scheme provided for the Tiv people. The Tivs offered an example of a self-contained community where Hausa was not used as a *lingua franca*. The Tivs, moreover, had provided a great number of recruits for the army during the war. Instruction in literacy was included amongst recommended methods for the resettlement of ex-servicemen and, fortunately, the *Gaskiya* Corporation was able to offer competent editorial work in the Tiv language. Where class and follow-up material was prepared for the literacy schemes in Hausa, limited editions in Tiv were also prepared, including a periodical in that language. When the Regional Adult Education Office was opened in 1949, the practice continued of collaboration with the Corporation, and the editors of the two periodicals—a Hausa and a Tiv respectively—were junior members of its editorial staff.

As work progressed towards a region-wide, intensive literacy campaign, there was opportunity to arrive at a more exact assessment of what would be required in the way of follow-up literature. Of all forms of publication, the newspaper recommended itself as the best for the purpose, for a number of reasons which will be mentioned in their proper places in the course of this survey. Active investigation and experiment soon indicated that a large number of separate local editions must be planned, in several different languages. Early in 1950, a target of fifteen separate editions was tentatively set for active planning with the prospect that more might be wanted, that modification to the territorial allocation for each edition might become necessary, but that ultimately local newspapers would emerge, printed and published locally, either officially or commercially. It was foreseen that the territorial distribution of these local newspapers would be automatically determined when the work of the intensive campaign, controlled from the centre, could be regarded as done.

For this project a good deal of language study was required, and also the recruitment and training of editorial staff who were natural speakers of the languages and dialects to be used. When the expanded Adult Education Headquarters was opened towards the end of 1952, the expatriate officer in charge of the Vernacular Literature Section took full control of editorial work on the periodicals. The Hausa and Tiv editors were seconded from the *Gaskiya* Corporation. Apprentice-editors for the new editions, as they came into being, were recruited locally by arrangement and sent direct to the Vernacular Literature Section on secondment from their native authorities, under whom they had been working as teachers or scribes. Keeping in view the requirements of literacy instruction, the incidence of bilingualism and the need for economy in printing costs, an orthographical survey was carried out with the assistance of an expert in linguistics supplied by UNESCO.*

Two other periodicals were started: a quarterly (subsequently monthly) magazine in English, of which a Hausa version was also issued; and a monthly supplement, in English, inserted by arrangement in the Hausa newspaper, *Gaskiya*. The English-language magazine, called *The World*, was intended for those who had received some education. It offered illustrated articles on scientific, geographical and historical subjects; general and practical hints; some fiction based on original contributions from readers; and literary and artistic competitions. The supplement to *Gaskiya*, which was called *The Leader*, was intended for those who wanted to improve their English, and offered general reading practice and formal study material. Publication of *The World* was made possible by a lady, the wife of a government official, who had experience of editorial work of this kind and of the special sort of rewriting necessary, and who was willing to undertake the whole task, including the collection of material and illustrations. *The Leader* was a routine production of the English Section attached to Adult Education Headquarters. When the English Section was absorbed into the Literature Agency, it took over the production of *The World* and issued *The Leader* for sale, separate from *Gaskiya*.

These periodicals will not be discussed in detail in this survey. They are mentioned here partly to complete the picture of the overall activities of the Agency, partly to emphasise the reliance that was placed on the periodical as a vehicle for enlightenment, but partly, also, to call attention to an aspect of the problem without some account of which the circumstances of the main task of literature production in Northern Nigeria cannot be fully understood. Put very briefly, there was no literature and no reading public already in existence which illiterates could hope to join when they became literate.

* Hans H. Wolff, *Nigerian Orthography*, North Regional Literature Agency, by arrangement with UNESCO.

A reading public had to be created which included not only the products of the literacy classes but also all those who had been to school or had become literate by any other means. There were no books in the vernaculars except school books, and in some languages not even these. The pitifully small circulation of *Gaskiya* showed that a great number of people who could have read it made no effort to do so. Not only were there literate products of primary schools without enough general knowledge and experience to be able to read it with intelligence, but there were also wide areas where Hausa was not understood and for which no alternative publication had been issued. By virtue of their literacy, people who had been to school found employment in central or local government departments and made no use other than professional of their literacy except, perhaps, as writers and readers of letters for illiterates. In their homes they shared the illiterate life of the community and lacked the opportunity, and in most cases the desire, to form a habit of reading either for pleasure or instruction. Exceptions to this generalisation could be found in individuals amongst those whose standard of education enabled them to find something to read in English, but the lack of local material separated them culturally from the community of their birth. *The World* failed to win a welcome from those for whom it was intended, namely, the young adults, including primary school teachers, who had learnt English at school, but did not keep up their reading in the language. It found its very limited market amongst senior school-children and students at training centres.

The main task of the Agency was to supply the present needs of the adult community as a whole for reading matter which was appropriate and topical for local preoccupations and interests. The vernacular news sheets set out to do this and to serve all literates, and not only those who had recently attended literacy classes. The original tentative estimate called for fifteen separate editions. By the end of 1956, thirteen were in being: eleven established and two still at the experimental stage. Six were in Hausa, with such differences of dialect as were necessary. This number included the parent paper, *Gaskiya*, which continued to be published for use in areas as yet without their own, and by Hausa colonies living in other regions of Nigeria and other African countries to whom copies were posted. The other editions were in Tiv, Kanuri, Fulani, Nupe, Yoruba, Igala and

Idoma respectively. Publication was fortnightly for established papers, but a monthly interval was allowed during the experimental period. The *Gaskiya* Corporation did the printing on the presses used for its own national Hausa and English newspapers, and approximately 75,000 copies of the complete series of vernacular news sheets were distributed each fortnight.

Each news sheet had its own editor, a natural speaker of the language used, born and brought up in the culture of the area in which it was distributed. Training was all 'on the job' and these editors were the first in the field as hitherto there had been no local papers and there was no local tradition for editorial work. Their educational background, like their ages, varied, but was relatively low. None had completed a full secondary-school course, though one or two may be said to have done the equivalent by attending training centres for junior primary-school teachers. In the circumstances this lack of higher education had its advantages, as their employment before their selection for trial as editors-in-training had not separated them from community life. Given normal intelligence, they could learn to make natural use of colloquial idiom in their work for the press. All had, at least, a smattering of English which increased as they went along, and most had, at least, some knowledge of Hausa, which quickly improved by their association in the editorial room and by their residence in a Hausa town. Their work was personally supervised by the editorial superintendent who was assisted by the man originally seconded from the staff of *Gaskiya* as editor of the parent Hausa news sheet. Periodically the editors were sent home to tour their areas, making contacts with readers and potential contributors, and consulting their native authorities in the interests of their papers. They were themselves, of course, well known at home. They had been selected for trial as editors from among the junior school teachers and scribes employed by the native authorities. In some cases, the first candidates sent on trial survived, but in others, there were one, two or even three changes before satisfactory editors were found. The practice was to stress their relationship with their native authorities, partly to make easy their reversion to their previous employment should they prove unsuitable as editors, partly to enlist the active interest of the native authority in the success of the news sheets, and partly with an eye to the future when publication could be undertaken locally and the men trained at the Agency would be required at home.

The functions of the news sheets were primarily to encourage reading, secondly to disseminate information, thirdly to introduce journalism as a local profession, and fourthly to foster indigenous talent for authorship. The daily life of the community provided the subject matter; the background to what was read was familiar, and accounts of other than local affairs were included only when they could be related directly to, or had a direct effect on, local preoccupations, and could be understood in terms of local experience. Information was factual, adding what was new to what was already known, and included when of topical interest and importance. The language used was idiomatic and conversational, and orthography was consistent. Information and advice on technical matters and public affairs had to derive from expert sources, but the copy that went to the press was written by a natural speaker of the language used.

The news sheets supported the general campaign for better living standards and the development of social institutions. The material was prepared in collaboration between the Agency and the various Ministries or other public bodies responsible for various aspects of public welfare and development. The material prepared might include posters, broadsheets, pamphlets and filmstrips in addition to the regular series of articles, special feature articles, notices and pictures which were prepared for the news sheets. All this material was complementary to the field-work which was the local expression of government policy for community development in its various aspects, and which the news sheets helped to explain.

Material of this kind requires lengthy forward preparation and must refer, therefore, to what can be foreseen far enough ahead to ensure topicality of publication. It must be related to long-term and routine programmes of activity. The news sheets were unsuitable for emergency propaganda, except when experts had deduced a strong possibility for which alternative material could be prepared in advance and used if required. Anticipatory action can be taken for those epidemics which seem to conform to patterns of frequency and movement, for invasions of locusts which may follow a course tentatively plotted by international organisations, and for developments in the field of national politics and local government which have been planned but of which the timing is uncertain. For these and other foreseeable possibilities, material could be ready for insertion when and if it became urgently topical.

Expert advice was directed towards what readers could do for themselves to raise their own standards of welfare and prosperity, and to contribute towards better standards of living and social organisation for the community in which they lived. Sectional and partisan controversy was avoided in the news sheets, which took no sides except to support expert knowledge against ignorance in the conduct of the practical activities of daily life.

A standard issue of any one of the news sheets contained local items, including news stories submitted by readers and official reports of public events received from local information officers; items of national and international affairs selected from the bulletins of official information services and the public press; expert advice and instruction dealing with such subjects as local agriculture, animal care, family welfare and health, thrift, local government and social development from authoritative sources; items of general knowledge and instruction in such matters as the use of postal services, prepared in collaboration with Adult Education Headquarters; public notices that were appropriate; readers' letters expressing opinions and asking questions of general interest; fables and original poetry submitted by or commissioned from members of the general public; puzzles and competitions; and editorial comment, written by the editor himself. This editorial comment was confined to two forms only: 1 a column in which he tried to put into perspective, in terms of local experience and understanding, important topical affairs reported elsewhere in the paper or any matter of general interest about which he felt he had something to say; and 2 such replies to readers' letters as might be needed.

Most of the material, it will be seen, came from outside, and the editors had little original writing to do. This little, however, was of great value and importance. Their work had to be supervised and scrutinised, and the editors required to check their opinions and knowledge from authoritative sources. Some editors learned more quickly, and some had greater natural gifts of expression than others; but it was found that, if the greatest possible freedom was allowed, editorial columns and comment not only appealed to readers as coming from writers who shared their patterns of thought and cultural experience, but also provided a yardstick with which to measure the level of understanding that could be expected from the readers. Apart from the routine business of mocking-up the paper and seeing it through the press, the main task of the editor lay in rewriting and preparing vernacular versions of the contents.

Most of the technical and welfare propaganda that was included was placed in a supplement printed in Hausa which formed the middle section of all the news sheets regardless of the language used for the rest of the paper. The practical reason for this arrangement was that the preparation of material of these specialised kinds in other languages would be too difficult while the apprentice-editors were new to their job. Its general justification was that, Hausa being the language of widest range, in most areas this material would appeal, in the first instance, to people with some education, most of whom would have picked up a working knowledge of Hausa at schools and central training institutions. Moreover, it was judged that the spread of Hausa as a *lingua franca* was desirable in the public interest. There was a move, however, towards the use of one language only throughout each paper, and the editors gained experience in the techniques of producing vernacular versions of material received in another language. Experience encouraged the rejection, on principle, of the bilingual periodical, and the number of literates who could and would benefit from reading material of this kind in their own language rapidly increased.

The task of the editor was to select items of local interest that came to hand and to amend, recast and rewrite them so that they were presented effectively in the standard colloquial form of the language or dialect, and to provide effective but accurate versions of official announcements and authoritative statements. Most local items came from readers whose letters ranged from semi-literate scrawl, which had to be deciphered, to well-written reports from better educated people. These latter, however, were often garrulous, and their letters were often in English or a *lingua franca* which, as a result of their schooling, they wrote more readily than their own language. All letters were carefully read and the suitability, authenticity and interest of their contents assessed. Versions for publication of those selected were then prepared. Great importance was attached to this role of readers in the production of the paper. Small fees in terms of the number of lines actually printed, regardless of the amount of rewriting that had been necessary, were sent to the originators. The hope was, of course, that they would observe the difference between what they wrote and what was printed, and that they would come to recognise the kind of story that was acceptable. Contributions of this kind were invited by announcements in the paper and by organisers of literacy schemes who constantly told people that anything worth remembering or worth telling other people was worth sending to their editor.

The editorial superintendent received official announcements from government, bulletins from regional, federal and Commonwealth information services, and source material from such international agencies as the United Nations, the World Health Organisation, and large commercial undertakings interested in the social advancement of the region. Specifically campaign material came from administrative, agriculture, health, veterinary, forestry and education officers by arrangement with their ministries. Military, police and postal authorities were consulted, and from time to time these sought the services of the Agency to publicise matters of interest to their undertakings.

Study and selection and collaboration with technical experts were sometimes done directly by the editorial superintendent, but sometimes by a senior officer of Adult Education Headquarters, who then collaborated with the editorial superintendent in the preparation of the programme for publication. Of the formidable amount and range of subject-matter indicated by the sources listed above, a very small amount indeed found its way into the news sheets whose aim was to emphasise only that which was immediately topical. The editorial superintendent was concerned also with the preparation and publication of posters for public display, booklets for public distribution and sale, and with discussion kits for groups and classes organised under Adult Education. In addition to editing their news sheets, editors were required to assist with the preparation of the different vernacular versions required for these other publications. Direct translation was not permitted, however well the editor might suppose he understood English or another vernacular in which the material had already been prepared. The editorial superintendent and one of his assistants discussed the subject-matter with the editor to ensure that he understood it correctly himself, and to seek its direct point of local application and the turn of phrase and the local allusion or popular proverb which could be used to fortify its message. During discussion local aspects of the matter would come to light, including popular misapprehensions, and these would suggest topics for editorial comment in the news sheet.

Ideally, every item included in issues of such news sheets should be carefully scrutinised and corrected to ensure its exact application to local circumstances and its exact aptitude of expression. But this is a counsel of perfection; all press work involves rush, and apprentice-editors make the mistakes of inexperience. Nevertheless if the principle holds for the main body of the contents where the editor and his readers share a common background of experience, it is still more applicable to the announcements of commercial advertisers that are accepted for publication. Apart from the revenue that advertisements bring to assist the cost of publication—which becomes a more important consideration when local papers are independently published—the inclusion of some advertising plays a part in the process of training people to edit and to read newspapers. The price paid in the world for agricultural raw products can mean that peasant farmers and their families have money to spend, and the market is potentially very great. It is part of the educational process towards higher standards of living that they should be given information about things on which they can usefully spend some of their money, and the opportunity to exercise discretion and selection in what they buy. It is right that the news sheets should carry advertiser's announcements but, where these papers are officially sponsored and their readers have come to regard their contents as well-intentioned in their interests, any advertisement included will be taken as carrying official approval and recommendation for the commodity advertised. It is no part of the campaign supported by the news sheets to encourage wasteful and harmful spending of money. Occasions may well arise when the papers may be used to issue warnings against the unreliability of some methods of advertising, yet advertisements accepted and paid for in the news sheets cannot be used as object lessons. The difficulty is to persuade suppliers and distributors of the right kind to buy the space and to accept advice on the manner in which their goods are advertised.

The process was begun of educating potential advertisers of repute as to the nature and size of the market, the value of the news sheets as vehicles for advertisement, and appropriate methods of advertising; and there was some encouraging response. Many branded commodities are of value to agriculture, and to health and family welfare. Their reliability can be checked with departmental experts. No purely local industries advertised; all advertisements came from large suppliers with international and world-wide coverage. The question of advertising was discussed with their local and touring representatives, and with visiting directors. An agent in London, who thoroughly understood the position, collaborated in the production of a printed folder which described the coverage offered and the terms, called attention to the need for specially designed and worded advertisements, and offered the editorial and artistic services of the Agency.

The style required for the wording of advertisements was the same as that required for the rest of the news sheet: the conversational style of the intelligent adult. The people who read our news sheets were masters of their own language, and what was said was what could be written and what could be read. Assistance to easy reading was given by editorial use of consistent orthography and punctuation, and by limiting each item to a single point of interest and keeping it as short as possible. New words come into a language with new ideas and new techniques, but they gain currency verbally and are as well known to illiterates as to literates, who share the same experience; and so the phonetic form which is coined in conversation can be included in publications without hesitation. Sometimes local associations provide new meanings for old words to express new ideas. An example of this is the use of the Hausa word *faifai*, which means a small round raffia mat used for covering food, for a gramophone record which the mat resembles in shape.

Slogans and telegraphese used in Western newspapers cannot be translated, nor should they or any other purely foreign idiom or convention be imitated. Headlines in the news sheets simply state the bare fact of what is to be described in detail underneath, or quote an appropriate proverb. The proverb, in fact, is the best local substitute for an advertiser's slogan. Captions to pictures must be long enough clearly to explain what is to be seen in the picture. Readers are learning to look at pictures for information, and appreciate instruction from the caption about what to look for in the picture. A caption can, with profit, be as long as an article in certain cases.

The standard vernacular news sheet had the shape and appearance of a 'tabloid' newspaper. It had eight pages of which the outer four were used for items of local interest and news stories contributed by readers, and the four inner pages formed a magazine section containing information and entertainment. Mention has already been made of this section as a supplement, in Hausa, issued with all local editions, and of the trend towards its modification to become an integral part of each local news sheet.

Each news sheet had its own title, locally chosen. This was printed boldly across the top of the front page, supported in some cases by symbolic devices of local significance. Four columns were used to each page so that larger type than was customary for newspapers could be used. Lines need to contain enough words to encourage smooth reading, and there must be a minimum of broken words at the end of lines, though, for adult readers, there is no need to eliminate these altogether. Experiment has shown that spacing is as important as size for legibility and that, for example, twelve point well-spaced and leaded to occupy the same area as fourteen point solid, is more legible. Straightforward roman type was used in the main, variety being given by using Gill sans-serif for some headlines and subtitles, and for some boxed announcements. Gill was also used for some picture-captions to provide clear distinction from neighbouring letter-press. Heavy and exaggerated types were not used, and headlines, which were sometimes rather lengthy, were no larger than was necessary clearly to separate item from item. All typographical problems were posed to the general manager of the *Gaskiya* Corporation, who arranged for specimens to be prepared exemplifying his professional advice, and from which selection could be made by eye.

The reproduction of photographs in newsprint is often disappointing but their inclusion was persevered with. Gradually local photographers learned to produce pictures of the right kind, editors became more experienced in selection, retouching became more skilful, and block-making and printing more efficient. Portraits of local notables reproduced well enough and were popular, but photographs were not as yet a satisfactory means of conveying information. Line drawings reproduced better, and were used for the cartoon type of illustration. The Agency employed a photographic technician, locally recruited though a native of another region, and a staff-artist who was a local man who had learnt 'on the job'. Two learner-artists were sponsored by the Agency for a course in commercial art organised at the local branch of the Nigerian College of Technology. Use was made of the work of freelance photographers and artists both of local and expatriate origin. A clear idea of the kind of illustration that was suitable was gained and the Agency was able to prepare the illustrations needed for its publications, including those required by advertisers.

The selling price of the news sheets was one penny. The Agency made no free issues, these being discouraged on principle with an eye to the future when commercial publishing should become a normal feature in a literate community. Losses incurred by the Agency were met from public funds.

When publication came under Adult Education, distribution was through official channels and normal government financial procedure was followed. This proved unsatisfactory and, when the Agency was opened, government provided for initial capital expenditure and made a trading fund available; thereafter the Distribution Section of the Agency, controlled by an experienced expatriate, used commercial business methods. Each of the twelve provinces of the Northern Region had a subdepot of the Agency to which was attached a three-ton van equipped as a bookshop which plied the main roads and market centres. One subdepot had a power launch to serve the area round the confluence of the Niger and Benue rivers. Bulk-supplies were forwarded by road or rail to the subdepots from headquarters, which also supplied direct the mission bookshops and the increasing number of private traders in all parts of the region who sold Agency publications on commission. Headquarters also dealt with a great number of individual mail orders both from within the region and from people of northern origin who lived in other regions and in other countries of Africa. In the Distribution Section and its subdepots local men were trained in the various branches of the book and periodical trade, both wholesale and retail.

The Agency, The *Gaskiya* Corporation, and Adult Education Headquarters were all sited close to each other at Zaria in Northern Nigeria. Their combined efforts were directed towards a time when a literate community would be competent to publish, print and market its own literature in its own idiom. The news sheets played their part, and the task was not to publish a periodical for people, but to train people to publish a periodical for themselves.

Early editions could be very slight. In communities where there is no existing literature and where the habit of reading has developed at no level, the practical advantage of being able to read tax-receipts and scales at produce-buying stations, and to read and write letters, is reward enough for the trouble taken in learning to be literate when the means are provided. The periodical is designed to foster the practice and enjoyment of reading for pleasure and self-instruction. The local newspaper, edited by a natural speaker of the language, offers the best form for this purpose because it contains a great number of items short enough to make for easy reading, and finds its subject-matter in what is familiar to the readers so that reading is related to real life. The language used is the idiom of uneducated adult conversation which, by its familiarity, helps to overcome the diffidence and difficulties of inexperienced readers.

This survey is based on the writer's direct observation of and participation in the literacy campaign described. The situation and policy outlined above are as he left them in 1956.

READING LIST

Although I believe this to be the first book which attempts to outline, for the general reader, the problem of illiteracy as it confronts the world in the second half of the century, a great deal has been written —especially since the Second World War—by and for those who are practically or politically involved in dealing with the problem.

A number of comprehensive bibliographies are available; I list some of these. There follow details, drawn from these bibliographies and from other sources, of books referred to in my text and of some others likely to be found useful by the reader desiring fuller information on various aspects of the problem. Several of the books thus listed contain bibliographies relevant to their particular subjects; these are marked by an asterisk (*).

Much of the material bearing on the problem is contained in articles scattered throughout a variety of periodicals. The bibliographies listed below give fuller references than would be practicable here, but I refer in the concluding section of this list to some of the periodicals in which such articles appear more or less regularly.

Unless otherwise stated, the place of publication of UNESCO works cited is Paris.

SELECTED BIBLIOGRAPHIES

du Sautoy, Peter, *Adult Literacy Education: Selected Bibliography*, Department of Adult Education, University of Manchester, Manchester 1966.

Ward, Betty A., *Literacy and Basic Elementary Education for Adults: A Selected Annotative Bibliography*, United States Office of Education, Bulletin No. 19, Washington DC 1961.

Alphabétisation et éducation des adultes en Afrique Noire et dans les pays en voie de développement: Choix de documents en lecture, Institut Pédagogique National, Paris 1965.

Literacy Education: A Selected Bibliography, UNESCO 1950.
Literacy Teaching: A Selected Bibliography, UNESCO 1956.

UNESCO PUBLICATIONS

1. Monographs on Fundamental Education

    X   Gray, William S., *The Teaching of Reading and Writing*, 1956.

    XI   *World Illiteracy at Mid-Century: A Statistical Study*, 1957.

  *XII Richards, Charles G. (ed.), *The Provision of Popular Reading Materials*, 1959.

2. Manuals on Adult and Youth Education

  *No. 2 Neijs, Karel, *Literacy Primers: Construction, Evaluation and Use*, 1961.

  *No. 3 Richards, Charles G. (ed.), *Simple Reading Material for Adults: Its Preparation and Use*, 1963.

  *No. 4 du Sautoy, Peter, *The Planning and Organization of Adult Literacy Programmes in Africa*, 1966.

  No. 5 Hely, A. S. M., *The School Teacher and Adult Education*, 1966.

3. Conference Documents and Reports

  ED/203   *Final Report of the Regional Conference on the Planning and Organization of Literacy Programmes in Africa*, 1964.

  ED/212   *Final Report of the Regional Conference on the Planning and Organization of Literacy Programmes in the Arab States*, 1964.

  13C/PRG/4 *General Conferences, 13th Session Programme Commission, World Literacy Programme*, 1964.

  ED/217   *Final Report of the World Conference of Ministers of Education on the Eradication of Illiteracy*, 1965.

  Minedlit 3 *Literacy as a Factor in Development*, 1965.

  Minedlit 5 *Statistics of Illiteracy*, 1965.

4. Reports and Papers on Mass Communication

  No. 22 *Periodicals for New Literates: Editorial Methods*, 1957.

  No. 24 *Periodicals for New Literates: Seven Case Histories*, 1957.

  No. 45 *Professional Training for Mass Communication*, 1965.

  No. 46 Lawrence, Robert de T., *Rural Mimeo Newspapers*, 1965.

5. General Material

Burnet, Mary, *ABC of Literacy*, 1965.
Escarpit, Robert, *La Révolution du livre*, 1965.
Hely, A. S. M., *New Trends in Adult Education*, 1962.
Oguzkan, Turhan, *Adult Education in Turkey*, 1955.
Spaulding, Seth, *Media Materials and Strategies in Literacy*, 1964.
The Development of Public Libraries in Africa, 1954.
World Press: Newspapers and News Agencies, 1964.

6. Periodicals

International Journal of Adult and Youth Education; quarterly.
Report of UNESCO Regional Centre for Reading Materials in South Asia, Karachi; quarterly.
UNESCO *Courier*; monthly.

Publications of National Governments

1. Cuba

Lorenzetto, Anna and Neijs, Karel, *Methods and Means Utilised in Cuba to Eliminate Illiteracy*, Ministry of Education, Havana 1965.
Ethiopia
The National Literacy Campaign in Ethiopia, National Literacy Campaign Organisation, Addis Ababa 1965.

3. France

Meyer, Jean, *Reflexions sur l'efficacité d'une action éducative concernant les adultes analphabètes*, Institut Pédagogique National, Paris 1963.
Alphabétisation et éducation des adultes en Afrique Noire et dans les pays en voie de développement, Institut Pédagogique National, Paris 1965.
Projet Gaston Berger: La Télévision au service de l'éducation, Institut Pédagogique National, Paris 1965.

4. Indonesia

Indonesia Free from Illiteracy, Djakarta 1965.

5. Mexico

Intensive Literacy Campaign, Ministry of Public Education, Mexico City 1965.

6. Soviet Union

Elimination of Illiteracy in USSR, Moscow n.d.
Aransky, V. et al., Reports prepared for Seminars for African

Planners and Organisers of Adult Literacy Programmes, Tashkent 1965, USSR Commission for UNESCO, Moscow 1965.

7. Sudan

Literacy and Illiteracy in the Sudan, Ministry of Education, Khartoum 1965.

8. United Kingdom

Community Development: A Handbook, HMSO, London 1958.

Report of Third Commonwealth Education Conference, Cmnd 2545, HMSO, London 1964.

9. United States

Murra, Kathrine O., *Sources of Information for Fundamental Education, With Special Reference to Education for Literacy*, Library of Congress, Washington DC 1948.

ACADEMIC AND UNOFFICIAL PUBLICATIONS

Curle, Adam, *World Campaign for Universal Literacy*, Center for Education and Development, Harvard University, Cambridge, Mass. 1963.

Gudschinsky, Sara, *Handbook of Literacy*, University of Oklahoma Press, Norman, Okla. 1953.

Hayes, Alfred S., *Recommendations of the Work Conference on Literacy held for the Agency of International Development* (May 23–28, 1964), Center for Applied Linguistics, Washington DC 1965.†

Hiebert, R. E. (ed.), *Books in Human Development*, Department of Journalism, The American University, Washington DC 1965.

Laubach, Frank Charles: (I) *India Shall Be Literate*, Mission Press, Jubbulpore 1940.

— (II)   *The Silent Billion Speak*, Friendship Press, New York 1945.

— (III) *Teaching the World to Read*, Lutterworth Press, London 1947.

— (IV)   *Towards World Literacy: The 'Each One Teach One' Way* (with Laubach, Robert S.), Syracuse University Press, Syracuse NY 1960.

Lewis, L. J. and Wrong, M., *Towards a Literate Africa*, Longmans, London 1948.

Maquerez, Charles, *La Promotion Technique du Travailleur Analphabète*, Eyrolles, Paris 1965.

† The Center for Applied Linguistics in Washington has begun a clearing house for world literacy documents, and distributes bibliographies and acquisition lists.

The Bethel Consultation on Christian Literature, 1962, Society for Promoting Christian Knowledge, London 1963.

PERIODICALS

Community Development Bulletin, University of London.
Community Development Journal, Didsbury, Manchester.
Coopération Pédagogique, Institut Pédagogique National, Paris.
Indian Journal of Adult Education, New Delhi.
Lit-Lit Newsletter, World Literacy and Christian Literature, New York.
Multiplier, The, Agency for International Development, Washington DC.
Newsletter, Laubach Literacy Fund Inc., Syracuse NY.
For UNESCO periodicals, see above; see also annual reports and newsletters of Bible and Missionary societies, e.g.:
American Bible Society, New York.
British and Foreign Bible Society, London.
Society for Promoting Christian Knowledge, London.
United Bible Societies, London.
United Society for Christian Literature, London.

REFERENCES

Unless otherwise stated, the publishing centre of UNESCO publications is Paris.

1. THE PROBLEM POSED

1. *World Illiteracy at Mid-Century: A Statistical Study*, Monographs on Fundamental Education No. XI, UNESCO 1957.
2. Prescott, William H., *The Conquest of Peru*, Swan Sonnenschein, London 1907, Vol. 1, p. 59.
3. Trevelyan, G. M., *English Social History*, Longmans, London and New York 1943, p. 264.
4. *World Illiteracy . . .*, pp. 22, 172, 103.
5. Information supplied by the United States Agency for International Development, Washington DC.
6. Burnet, Mary, *The ABC of Illiteracy*, UNESCO 1965, p. 19.
7. *Illiteracy Spells Hunger*, reprinted from UNESCO *Courier*, February 1963, p. 2.
8. Gray, William S., *The Teaching of Reading and Writing*, Monographs on Fundamental Education No. X, UNESCO 1956, p. 24.
9. *Lit-Lit Newsletter*, organ of the Committee on World Literacy and Christian Literature, New York, September 1965.

2. SOUND AND SYMBOL

1. Wilson, R. A., *The Miraculous Birth of Language*, 1927; rev. edn, Guild Books, London 1941, p. 178.
2. Laubach III: Frank Charles Laubach, *Teaching the World to Read*, Lutterworth Press, London 1947, p. 54.
3. Shaw, George Bernard, in Preface to 1941 edn of Wilson, op. cit., p. 27.
4. Hogben, Lancelot, *From Cave Painting to Comic Strip*, Max Parrish, London 1949, p. 89.

192

5. Laubach III, p. 63.
6. Ibid., p. 62.
7. Hogben, op. cit., p. 127.

3. THE MAP OF ILLITERACY

1. Minedlit 5: *Statistics of Illiteracy*, UNESCO memorandum for the Teheran Conference, 1965, p. 2.
2. Minedlit 3: *Literacy as a Factor in Development*, UNESCO memorandum for the Teheran Conference, 1965, p. 8.
3. Minedlit 5, p. 7.
4. Minedlit 3, p. 8.
5. Mendelssohn, Kurt, "China's Cultural Revolution", *The Listener*, London, December 8, 1966.
6. Annual Report of the British and Foreign Bible Society, London 1963, p. 72.
7. *Population Profile*, Population Reference Bureau Inc., Washington DC, September 26, 1966, p. 3.
8. *World Illiteracy . . .*, p. 130.

4. PIONEER ATTACKS ON ILLITERACY

1. Laubach III, p. 121.
2. *Elimination of Illiteracy in USSR*, Moscow n.d., p. 7.
3. Aransky, V., *State Bodies and Public Organisations in the Elimination of Illiteracy in USSR*, USSR Commission for UNESCO, Moscow 1965, pp. 4-5.
4. *Elimination . . .*, p. 10.
5. Laubach II: Frank Charles Laubach, *The Silent Billion Speak*, Friendship Press, New York 1945, p. 27.
6. Ibid., p. 70.
7. Ibid., p. 196.
8. Laubach I: Frank Charles Laubach, *India Shall Be Literate*, Mission Press, Jubbulpore 1940, p. 7.

5. MID-CENTURY EXPERIMENTS

1. Coomassie, Mallam Ahmadu, paper prepared for the International Seminar on Adult Education in Changing Africa, Accra 1955.
2. *World Illiteracy . . .*, p. 38.

3. Minedlit 5, p. 25.
4. Meyer, Jean, in *Coopération Pédagogique*, French Ministry of Education, Paris, October–December 1964.
5. Laubach II, p. 195.
6. Lorenzetto, Anna and Neijs, Karel, *Method and Means Utilised in Cuba to Eliminate Illiteracy*, UNESCO report published by the Cuban Ministry of Education, Havana 1965.
7. Ibid., p. 73.

6. UNESCO TAKES A HAND

1. *World Illiteracy* . . ., p. 5.
2. ED/203: *Final Report of the Regional Conference on the Planning and Organization of Literacy Programmes in Africa*, UNESCO 1964, p. 2.
3. General Assembly Resolution 1677, Session 1961–62.
4. *A Decisive Step for a World Campaign against Illiteracy*, reprinted from UNESCO *Chronicle*, January 1964, p. 2.
5. Ibid., p. 4.
6. Ibid., p. 4.
7. 13C/PRG/4: *World Literacy Programme*, report to the General Conference, 13th session, Programme Commission, UNESCO 1964, p. 1.
8. Ibid., p. 5.
9. ED/203, p. 35.
10. Cmnd 2545: Report of the Third Commonwealth Education Conference, Ottawa 1964, HMSO, London 1964, p. 74.
11. Ibid., p. 75.
12. Ibid., p. 76.
13. Hayes, Alfred S. (ed.), *Recommendations of the Work Conference on Literacy*, Center for Applied Linguistics, Washington DC 1965, pp. 18–20.
14. Ibid., p. 9.
15. Ibid., p. 39.

7. TEHERAN—A TURNING POINT?

1. 13C/PRG/4, p. 1.
2. Ibid., p. 9.

3. ED/212: *Final Report of the Regional Conference on the Planning and Organization of Literacy Programmes in the Arab States*, UNESCO 1964.
4. WS/0465 EDA: *Guide for the Preparation of Experimental Literacy Projects*, UNESCO, April 16, 1965.
5. Burnet, op. cit., p. 63.
6. Minedlit 5, p. 7.
7. Minedlit 3, p. 11.
8. Ibid., p. 14.
9. Ibid., p. 16.
10. Ibid., pp. 23–4.
11. Ibid., p. 39.
12. Ibid., p. 39.
13. ED/217: *Final Report of the World Conference of Ministers of Education on the Eradication of Illiteracy, at Teheran*, UNESCO 1965, p. 32.
14. Ibid., p. 33.
15. Cf. *The Multiplier*, International Co-operation Administration, Washington DC, July–August 1961.
16. For details of the French system see Hayter, Teresa, *French Aid*, Overseas Development Institute, London 1966.

8. ORGANISATION OF LITERACY PROGRAMMES

1. ED/217, p. 40.
2. Minedlit 3, p. 21.
3. du Sautoy, Peter, *The Planning and Organization of Adult Literacy Programmes in Africa*, Manuals on Adult and Youth Education No. 4, UNESCO 1966, p. 51.
4. Laubach I, p. 44.
5. Coomassie, op. cit.
6. ED/217, p. 30.
7. Burnet, op. cit., pp. 27–34.
8. Laubach III, p. 67.
9. Laubach I, p. 93.
10. Ibid., p. 87.
11. Burnet, op. cit., p. 18.

9. TEACHING PEOPLE TO READ

1. Laubach I, p. 19.
2. Ibid., pp. 52–9.
3. Neijs, Karel, *Literacy Primers: Construction, Evaluation and Use*, Manuals on Adult and Youth Education No. 2, UNESCO 1961, pp. 15, 23.
4. Ibid., p. 14.
5. Meyer, op. cit., p. 23.
6. Neijs, op. cit., p. 100.
7. du Sautoy, op. cit., p. 91.

10. READING MATERIAL FOR NEW READERS

1. Laubach III, p. 162.
2. Richards, Charles G. (ed.), *The Provision of Popular Reading Materials*, Monographs on Fundamental Education No. XII, UNESCO 1959, p. 5.
3. Ibid., p. 26.
4. Ibid., pp. 213–33.
5. Cf. Griffin, Ella, "Popular Reading Materials for Ghana", *International Journal of Adult and Youth Education*, UNESCO, No. 3, 1965.
6. Richards, Charles G. (ed.), *Simple Reading Material for Adults: Its Preparation and Use*, Manuals on Adult and Youth Education No. 3, UNESCO 1963, p. 27.
7. du Sautoy, op. cit., p. 84.
8. Lawrence, Robert de T., *Rural Mimeo Newspapers*, Reports and Papers on Mass Communication No. 46, UNESCO 1965, p. 12.

11. MATERIAL FOR MATURE READERS

1. Richards, *Provision . . .*, p. 68.
2. *World Press*, UNESCO 1964, p. 13.
3. Ibid., p. 90.
4. Hiebert, R. E. (ed.), *Books in Human Development*, Department of Journalism, The American University, Washington DC 1965, p. 11.
5. Ibid., p. 73.

6. Cf. *The Bethel Consultation on Christian Literature*, Record of Proceedings, October 8–13, 1962, Society for Promoting Christian Knowledge, London 1963, p. 62.
7. Hiebert, op. cit., pp. 80–1.
8. *Illiteracy Spells Hunger*, p. 2.

12. DISTRIBUTION

1. Richards, *Provision* . . ., pp. 32–7.

13. 'A SOLEMN AND URGENT APPEAL'

1. Minedlit 5.
2. *World Illiteracy* . . ., p. 165
3. Cmnd 2545, p. 74.
4. *Population Profile*, p. 1.
5. Laubach II, p. 201.
6. *World Illiteracy* . . ., p. 99.
7. Visser 't Hooft, W. A., "Material Need as a Spiritual Concern", *The Listener*, London, March 16, 1967, p. 358.
8. ED/217, pp. 22–3.

INDEX